CONFESSIONS OF A FOOTBALL REPORTER ... ANOTHER BIGGS AT LARGE

Alan Biggs

CONFESSIONS OF A FOOTBALL REPORTER . . . ANOTHER BIGGS AT LARGE

Alan Biggs

Vertical Editions

www.verticaleditions.com

First published in the United Kingdom in 2011 by Vertical Editions, Unit 4a, Snaygill Industrial Estate, Skipton, North Yorkshire BD23 2QR

www.verticaleditions.com

ISBN 978-1-904091-51-6

A CIP catalogue record for this book is available from the British Library

Cover design by HBA, York

Printed and bound by Jellyfish Print Solutions, Hampshire

ACKNOWLEDGEMENTS

To six friends for their great support for this project. To Grahame Lloyd and Lance Hardy, published authors both, for their expert advice; to Trevor Francis for honouring me with such a generous foreword; to artist Pete McKee and photographer Trevor Smith for their talent and flair . . . and to Tony Hallam, a former schoolteacher who, on hearing a talk I gave, inspired the idea to write this book at a time when I had never given it a thought.

To Lynne, Ashley, Rosanna and Isabelle. For all their love, encouragement . . . and patience.

CONTENTS

FOREWORD

It's a popular perception that there are running battles between managers and journalists. That is true in some cases but there are many others where good relationships are formed.

So it was with Alan Biggs during my time with Sheffield Wednesday, first as a player and then for four years as manager. Alan was one of several journalists over that period who I came to trust. I think my involvement working with the media from such a young age helped me to have a greater appreciation and understanding. Hillsborough was a happy period for all of us in that the local reporters, unaccustomed to success, enjoyed the good times almost as much as the players and fans.

Stepping up to take over from Ron Atkinson in 1991 gave me a very hard act to follow. Wednesday had been promoted back to the top flight and won the League Cup the previous season. I was able to maintain the momentum with much the same side to start with before building on it over time with the signing of top players like Chris Waddle and Des Walker. Qualification for Europe was achieved through finishing third in my first season and reaching the final of both domestic cups in 1993.

Despite not having the financial resources of some of the bigger clubs we continued to progress and competed at a high level in the top flight. I felt Alan showed a very intelligent grasp of the job I was trying to do. He would analyse my difficulties, especially in the *Sheffield Telegraph* where his articles put across certain points to supporters that I much appreciated.

During my time at Wednesday there were one or two minor disagreements with Alan which is inevitably the case, but I felt he was always fair and balanced, particularly towards the latter part of my time in Sheffield. Those were difficult days because I virtually knew my fate weeks in advance, but I felt Alan and his colleagues respected the dignified way I tried to behave.

Overall, my spell in Sheffield was the most enjoyable period of my career. I especially remember the rivalry with Sheffield United's manager of the time, Dave Bassett. I didn't know him before I took the job and we were seen as total opposites. But there was a chemistry between us when we met and our close friendship has lasted to this day.

Journalists have a difficult job which, I suppose, is sometimes not recognised by many of those in the game and outside it. I'm sure this memoir will provide a revealing insight from the other side of the fence. As usual, I know that Alan will have set out to present a fair and honest account, and as a good friend I would like to wish him every success with the book.

Trevor Francis
England's first £1m player, former England striker, European Cup winner and currently a much respected television pundit.

PROLOGUE

Everyone's heard of Ronnie Biggs. Not so Alan Biggs. We're no relation, by the way, and were never acquainted, either, I should add. Otherwise, 'Uncle Ronnie', as my family has often referred to the Great Train Robber, would definitely be in this book. You see, some journalists become better known than many of the stars they interview. Then there are the also-rans who resort to namedropping. And I make no apologies for being shamelessly among them . . . because it might be the only way to encourage you to read what follows!

That's a journalist for you, always needing an angle to get people hooked. So let me take you through the maze of my media career, primarily as a football writer and broadcaster, with the help of the host of household names I have encountered along the way. The cast includes Trevor Francis, Dave Bassett, Neil Warnock and Chris Waddle. And starring roles, too, for greats from other sports like Fred Trueman, Geoffrey Boycott, Dickie Bird and Seb Coe.

From making a radio debut at Wembley to interviewing ex-Beatle George Harrison . . . from broadcasting weather reports from a hot air balloon to being barred by football hardman Ken Bates . . . and from scrapes with Jack Charlton and Ron Atkinson to casting light on the one of the faceless men who run English football . . . it's hard to take much of it too seriously. But what a life of fun, literally never a dull moment. Time I tried to share it with someone, with the promise that it doesn't really matter if you've never heard of the author.

A pocket of the population may have come across me reporting on football over the last 30-odd years—for national radio and television, and in newspapers. Lots of stories come from that field and other sports. But it's not just football. This is meant as a light-hearted insight into our mad media existence; the tightrope we walk, the rows and reconciliations, the many things that can and do go wrong.

Don't worry. This is nothing so grand as an autobiography. Look at it as a collection of true-life tales from somewhere outside of the real world . . . by someone who has never had a proper job.

1

STONE THE CROWS—
I'M AT WEMBLEY!

A local newspaper office in 1974. We're talking before *The Sweeney*, *Life on Mars* and *Ashes to Ashes*. Cops behaved differently then and so did hacks. But we didn't attack anything unless it was pints of bitter. A liquid lunch was as essential as a notebook and pen. Afternoons were distinctly blurred round the edges.

It was during one such hazy afternoon, while working as a trainee reporter on the *Derbyshire Times* in Chesterfield, that I found myself with two contrasting articles on the go. One was an obituary on the death of a local dignitary. The other was a slightly amusing tale about the theft of a weighty stone scarecrow from somebody's garden. All seemed to be going to plan. I'd interviewed the son of the dignitary in my most respectful tones and had also talked, with rather more levity, to the erstwhile owner of the stone scarecrow. Stones bitter—the office's favoured lunchtime tipple—becomes more relevant at this point.

Having dealt with the obit, I came to writing up the scarecrow story and realised, not for the first time or the last, that I was missing a vital detail. So I reached for my notebook, dialled one of the two telephone numbers listed and breezily intoned: 'Sorry to bother you again, it's the *Derbyshire Times* . . . how much did your scarecrow weigh?'

You'll have guessed where I inadvertently placed that call—and what happened next. A long pause was followed by an explosion of indignation down the phone. A blurting out from the bereaved son that 'Your editor will be hearing about this' and a slamming down of the receiver. Barely five minutes later, recoiling in horror, I was being summoned to the office of Mr Humphrey Oliver. Fortunately for me, Humphrey was a kindly old soul. I was much relieved that he fielded the complaint rather than his feared deputy. Humphrey did his best to give me a good ticking off but I swear I saw his military moustache quiver in suppressed mirth as he showed me the door—but stopped short of bundling me through it on this occasion.

That was to come a few months later. The *Derbyshire Times* (or DT as we called it) operated a Dickensian regime in everything bar their attitude to long lunches and it was only the shared misery with colleagues like Graham Bannister, a lifelong pal, that kept me sane. In turn, the paper was only too happy to release me from my indentures. This, by the way, was an apprenticeship and nothing to do with oral hygiene—except that my bosses undoubtedly felt that training me was a bit like pulling teeth. They cheerfully waved me off to join a two-bit television outfit called *Sheffield Cablevision* . . . where I had actually been moonlighting for some weeks. I would race off to Sheffield early on a Friday evening to present a weekend sports preview for the 30,000 households subscribing to an experimental piped TV channel.

My cover was blown on a Friday when Sheffield United were playing and I had arranged to meet a good pal, Bernard Jones, for a pre-match drink near Bramall Lane. Bernard, a DT photographer, just happened to walk past the only television shop in Sheffield city centre that showed Cablevision. It also happened to be during the five minutes that I was on screen. Bernard told me he sort of turned into a cartoon character. He walked past, stopped, did a double-take and looked back into the window in astonishment. 'I knew it was you because your tie was all over the place like it was in the pub at lunchtime,' said Bernard, who couldn't wait to relate his discovery when we met. He kept it quiet like I asked but somehow the word got round. It's a bit hard to keep a secret that you are sharing with a few thousand people and I was truly naïve to think otherwise.

Luckily, Cablevision's boss John Brand—to whom I owe a big debt of thanks for introducing me to broadcasting—offered me a job in the nick of time. Instead of facing the sack, I was able to save the DT the trouble by resigning. Cablevision was much more fun, even though it lasted only another five months after I joined as sports editor (no coincidence perhaps!) But it was long enough for me to begin my career as a serial namedropper.

My most prized interview during that time was with the then England cricket captain, Tony Greig. How I managed to get this interview might impress you more. It was during a Test match against Australia at nearby Headingley in Leeds. Note not *after* but *during*. The protocol then was that captains and players generally said next to nothing while the game was in progress. So how did we extract this gem? It was ridiculously simple. We just drove up to Leeds in the station's clapped-out outside broadcast van, blagged our way into the ground and fetched Greig out onto the field. Yes, really!

These days all manner of advanced notice, signed in triplicate, would be required. Instead, I simply strolled into the pavilion, asked to speak to Tony Greig, waited for him to appear and persuaded him to join me in front of our cameras. No money changed hands, no pre-arrangement was needed, only a polite request obligingly answered. How simple life was in 1975.

The problem was that our coup—to be broadcast the next day to coincide with a major pitch for advertisers—was rudely upstaged and rendered meaningless by the 'Free George Davis' brigade. Some may remember how, in campaigning for the release of a convicted robber, the gang broke into Headingley overnight (if I could, they could!) and poured oil on the pitch to scupper the game and draw attention to their cause. Davis was subsequently released when the case was reviewed but was then jailed for 15 years in 1978. Anyway, we weren't going to let his supporters stop us even though the match itself was abandoned. We ran the tape regardless, despite it having little relevance to the big news of the day.

We did have one or two genuine triumphs, for instance getting the first interview with the next incoming manager of Sheffield United, Jimmy Sirrel. That involved a late afternoon dash to Meadow Lane, where Jimmy was still working for Notts County, and a rush-hour race from Nottingham to Sheffield city centre in 50 minutes flat. You try it! With news editor Nick Smart at the wheel of his Volkswagen Beetle, we got the tape on the six-o'clock news magazine with minutes to spare. I also recall interviewing cricketing great Frank Woolley—much to the pride and delight of my father, John, who grew up idolising the legendary former Kent and England all-rounder as a fan of the county.

Equally memorable were various encounters with a celebrity clairvoyant called Simon Alexander. I dreamt up a stunt for him whereby I smuggled him into Hillsborough to film an attempt to lift a supposed curse from Sheffield Wednesday—who were in an even sorrier state then than they have been in more recent times. Unfortunately, our outdated mobile camera—like a very primitive camcorder—caught the curse and failed to record. Nevertheless, other media outlets jumped on the story and Simon was invited up to Leeds for a live interview with *BBC Look North*. Sadly—because of the recording glitch—I had to persuade him to stay put to make a live appearance with me before a fraction of the audience in Sheffield (it was my idea, after all).

Simon was not best pleased. He got his chance for revenge soon afterwards when I playfully challenged his mystical claims over a beer at our local. His response was to tell me he would stop the circulation in my right leg. And he did. Or at least that's how it felt. Terrifyingly, my leg went deathly cold and I found myself pleading with him to stop. All in the mind, of course, but it worked on me.

Pity Simon wasn't around to help one day when a taped

programme failed during transmission, as was often the case. In that event, the nearest available presenter would be bundled into the tiny continuity studio to talk his head off to camera until the machine was fixed. This day it was my turn only to discover that somebody had nicked the chair. So I had to crouch down with my back against the wall with my head and shoulders in line with the fixed camera . . . and waffle on seemingly comfortably about things I could remember to trail about upcoming programmes . . . while at the same time performing a very difficult and painful endurance exercise. I don't know at what point my fixed grin turned into a grimace, but I do know I was mightily relieved to finally get the thumbs-up from next door that the tape was ready to roll.

The head of Cablevision, John Brand, was a colourful character, a one-time actor and voiceover specialist who was the man who proudly proclaimed Wilkinson Sword as 'the name on the world's finest blade'. He could also lacerate with his tongue, aided and abetted by his deep, rich, rumbling delivery. John's language was fruity at the best of times—but woe betide anyone who swore within range of a microphone. That was a golden rule I have never forgotten, even in the most trying circumstances. For some reason, John saw broadcasting promise in me and I'll always be grateful for that.

Looking back, to call Cablevision toytown TV is a slightly cruel assessment, especially as I should be so grateful to the pioneers who ran it. They believed in what was a community project and, on reflection, it wasn't a world away from today's so-called reality stuff in that volunteers could come in off the street to help us make programmes.

I doubt today's ef'n'safety police would have been too impressed, though. Part of my dubious job description involved trailing camera cables precariously through catwalks under the then decrepit roof of Sheffield's Owlerton Stadium from where we covered speedway. At one point I nearly fell through the floor—or ceiling—into the lounge bar below. Not that my more technically minded colleagues were sympathetic. They fell about one day when I completed my hazardous crawl only to poke the wrong end of the cable through the loop hole in the far corner of the stand roof—and had to do the job all over again. Years later, at a reunion dinner, they presented me with a dubious trophy—the mounted end of a camera cable!

Even the Cablevision studio wasn't safe, as one guest in particular was to discover. I was halfway through interviewing Radio Hallam's sports editor Stuart Linnell when both of us were stunned into silence by what sounded like a gunshot. In fact, a studio light—and they were fiercely hot in those days—had exploded. Later, I discovered a singed bullet-sized hole in my rollneck sweater—evidence of a lucky escape from red hot flying glass. Thankfully, Stuart was also unscathed—because he became my mentor.

Our first contact had been equally accidental. It was during my last couple of months at the DT soon after Radio Hallam's launch as the exciting new commercial sound of South Yorkshire and North Derbyshire. Stuart needed outside help for football coverage and enlisted two of my far more senior colleagues on the paper, Barrie Farnsworth and John Smith. I was envious to say the least, trying hard not to let it show. No-one could have foreseen the events that saw me cover my very first game on radio—at Wembley stadium. And a game that would bring me into contact with Peter Swan, one of the three footballers jailed following a notorious bribes scandal in 1964. Swan was player-manager of non-league Matlock Town who made a surprise run to the final of the FA Trophy in 1975. John Smith had been Hallam's reporter in the later rounds and naturally was Stuart's choice for the final. But John, as a Matlock supporter, simply wanted to enjoy the day. His 19-year-old stand-in will forever be grateful to him for that.

The only thing wrong with that springtime afternoon at the home of football was that my career has been going downhill ever since! It was some debut, though. Matlock beat Scarborough 4–0, I managed to identify all their players even though three of them were lookalike brothers (Tom, Nick and Mick Fenoughty) and I couldn't have cared less that I ended up out of pocket for the trip. Let me explain how.

Obviously Stuart wanted an after-match interview, a standard request then as now. What has changed so much is that my only broadcast tool that day was a landline telephone in the press box right up in the gods. So getting Peter Swan up there was really more of a job for Captain Kirk on *Star Trek*. Added to which there was not even a lift for most of the way up. The only way was via a confusing, labyrinthine route which involved multiple staircases and required a degree in orienteering. And remember that Swanny was by this time a veteran player. Yes, he was euphoric but he was also exhausted. I had to kid him he didn't have far to go to the press box but halfway up one flight of stairs, he wearily turned to me and said: 'Is there a payment for this interview?'

Realising that the success or failure of my mission depended on the answer, I fished a fiver out of my pocket and asked if that would do. Peter simply plodded on. I laugh when people hearing this story point out the irony of me having to 'bribe' him. Seriously, I can't blame Swanny who I found in many subsequent—entirely free—interviews to be a really likeable, honest bloke who openly regretted his one major mistake in life. Besides, he wasn't to know that he had taken nearly half my match fee. It was just £11 a game in those days, if I recall correctly. And I should do because just a few years later, as Radio Hallam's sports editor myself, I was working to such a strict budget that I had to perpetuate those frugal rates.

Incidentally, the drama didn't end with Peter's live down-the-phone chat with Stuart. The pair of us got totally lost on our way down from the press box and several newspaper reporters were moaning about a frustratingly long wait for their quarry by the time I found us the exit. One of them, the late Benny Hill (no, not that one—but this guy was an even funnier character, believe me) used the delay spectacularly to his advantage with an intro to his story that has stuck with me ever since. Recalling that Swan's last appearance for England at the stadium had been in 1962 (ahead of his long ban), Benny wrote: 'It has taken Peter Swan 13 years to get back into Wembley . . . and when he finally made it on Saturday his biggest problem was trying to get out of the place.'

Radio Hallam was where it was at in Sheffield's media scene around the mid-1970s. The station boasted household names in BBC radio broadcasting like Roger Moffat, Keith Skues, Johnny Moran and Bill Crozier. Little did I imagine that I would be working in such elite company. But Stuart Linnell gave me the chance to do a bit of freelancing for the station while I was still employed by Cablevision . . . things like reading racing results, covering a tennis tournament and, ridiculously as it now seems, reporting on a Subbuteo competition! All a bit of a comedown from Wembley as I did my apprenticeship in reverse. I would also contribute a weekend non-league preview on a Friday show presented by former Sheffield Wednesday and Hull player Ken Knighton. Michael Morgan, then of the *Daily Express* and subsequently a close colleague for many years, would give his opinions on the big stuff.

After promptings from Stuart, a one-man band who needed inside help on sport, Hallam's news editor Ian Rufus was persuaded (to his understandable and later regret, I thought at times) to offer me a job as a news reporter on the station. Frankly, my heart wasn't in it at first. I have to admit my attitude was slovenly—by contrast with my enthusiastic contributions from Bramall Lane and Hillsborough. Ian sorted me out with a timely and well deserved rollocking.

Although I still fell short on drive at times, I had learned a valuable lesson about professionalism and what it means. I discovered that doing a job thoroughly is a cause for satisfaction in itself regardless of whether you find it stimulating. Ian recognised the improvement and promoted me to morning editor with responsibility for presenting the station's peaktime bulletins—in place of Martin Kelner, who switched to presentation duties and is now a well-known broadcaster and satirist. One downside was that I had to get up at quarter to five every morning . . . and if there was a game to cover that night I would end up working right through. Needless to say, this would seem to have required some curtailing of my social habits—a sacrifice that, at 22, I simply refused to make! Disguising the fact that I was bleary-eyed and hung over somehow became an enjoyable challenge, even a source of fun.

Not that this could explain one of the most mysterious incidents of my life and something that still sends a chill up my spine to this day. It had nothing to do, either, with a hair-raising hot air balloon adventure. I'll come to that shortly. Among Hallam's big-name presenters was Bruce Wyndham, a former BBC stalwart recruited to join old cronies like best pal Moffat. Unbeknown to me, after I had clocked off for the day one lunchtime, Bruce sadly collapsed and died at the station while preparing for a programme. There was no immediate announcement and I was none the wiser.

The following morning, I awoke to my jangling alarm with a vivid dream running through my head. I was reading the news and relaying the death of someone with the initials BW. For some reason, I felt under particular pressure to make sure I read this right. The only BW I could think of was the then England cricketer Bob Willis. No, surely not. So I put the dream out of my mind as I drove to work . . . until arriving at my desk to pick up Sheffield's *Morning Telegraph* newspaper. That was always the first thing I did.

There on the front page was a picture of Bruce Wyndham. It wasn't uncommon to see my celebrity colleagues in the paper. 'What's Bruce been up to,' I thought. . . and then I read the headline. 'DJ dies.' I was stunned, of course, besides being upset by the news. But even then I didn't register the significance of my dream. It only dawned on me when I was in the studio reading the item that devastated everyone who knew Bruce, a lovely cheerful character who would always crack a joke at his own expense. Explain that one. I can't. I have always had an open mind about the paranormal and, although nothing like this has happened to me since, I can't help wondering if I received something other than radio waves that day.

2

UP, UP AND AWAY . . .

'Everybody off . . . get off the field now, please.' This was the command from ace hot air balloon pilot Robin Batchelor, as recorded by yours truly, at the end of a memorable Saturday afternoon flight over Sheffield. Figures in white scattered in all directions as we landed on a cricket ground in the middle of a game. And the field was then engulfed by a couple of hundred kids who had evidently tracked our progress while I did a series of live reports from high over the city. Belated apologies to the cricketers we rudely interrupted. But at least they could make a unique entry to the scorebook: balloon stopped play. Had this been a first-class game, it would have ranked even higher than the 'snow stopped play' announcement from a Derbyshire game at Buxton in 1975 after an inch of the stuff fell in early June.

I couldn't have envisaged such a whacky summer's afternoon when I finished my morning news shift. In fact, I was halfway out the door when I fielded a phone call from the State Express cigarette company. They said they had their hot air balloon parked in the centre circle at Bramall Lane football ground. Would anyone from the station like to join them for a pleasure flight? Stuart Linnell, about to take the airways for a rather flat summer sports show, pricked up his ears. And that's how I came to present weather forecasts from 1,000 feet above Sheffield city centre.

'It's pretty calm up here but there's plenty of turbulence in my stomach . . .' was how I summed up. In fact, the scariest bit was suddenly finding myself level with the top of the floodlight pylons at Bramall Lane. I felt like crouching down in the basket at that point and it was a while before I dare look over the side.

Any pride I feel about that adventure is all to do with the identity of the pilot. Robin Batchelor was unknown at that point but has since become quite famous for taking part in several daredevil japes with Sir Richard Branson, including an attempt to cross the Atlantic. In fact, it was Robin who taught Branson to fly. More recently, he has featured in television series with actor Stephen Tompkinson, flying over South Africa and Australia. And I know from my own experience that he can be a bit of a risk-taker who's never happier than when literally flying by the seat of his pants.

On that memorable day, we were over built-up Sheffield (at a lower altitude than officially permitted, as he freely confessed to me at the time!) when he casually announced that we were running out of fuel and needed to land. As the ground started to rise up to meet us Robin's eyes alighted on the sports field . . . and the rest is history in the annals of Sheffield league cricket.

My weather reports were only possible through walkie-talkie devices that were bulky to carry and squawky to hear. I hated them up to that point, not least because mine had come to life with a series of loud squelches in a message from my boss right in the middle of a Sheffield council meeting. And I didn't know how to turn the damn thing off. I was ordered to make that discovery in the corridor outside!

Another voice that came through loud and clear during this time was that of Hallam's deputy news editor Jim Greensmith. Again it was a Saturday, only this was at 5.30 in the morning at the start of my shift. Normally I saw and heard no-one but the duty presenter. This time Jim's disembodied voice came floating into the newsroom, calling me by name. But where was he and how could I reply? Eventually I found the right button on the console to discover that Jim was out in the radio car . . . at the scene of a mass murder. If you remember the grisly events at Pottery Cottage at

Eastmoor near Chesterfield, where four people were killed in January 1977, then you'll know that this was a major national story. Billy Hughes, the murderer, was eventually shot dead by police after a car chase in Cheshire.

Thanks to Jim, who was to become a police media spokesman before sadly dying of a brain tumour, our contacts with the force were excellent. One particularly helpful officer was David Duckenfield who was later one of the police chiefs under fire during inquiries into the Hillsborough disaster. Whatever the rights and wrongs surrounding that tragic event, I felt terribly sorry for David who I found to be a thoroughly likeable and helpful guy. With all due sympathy and respect to the many bereaved families, I can't help feeling there is too much of a blame culture in society. All of us are subject to human error but most of us are fortunate to do jobs where one mistake, honestly made, does not have life-or-death consequences.

Another particularly kindly cop was Kenneth Unwin who was in charge of the Chesterfield division and had a great sense of humour. Once I had to ad-lib a live interview with him during a news bulletin and drew a complete blank on his Christian name. It came to me at the last second—or so I thought. 'We go now to Chesterfield police superintendent . . . er . . . Stanley Unwin.' Stanley Unwin was, of course, a famous comedian who invented his own language, a mangled form of English. Ken was such a good sport he carried on regardless and settled for pulling my leg about it later.

Besides assisting with enquiries, Ken would invite you to police social events and if you happened to see him out, he'd insist on buying you a pint. I'd often refuse on the diplomatic grounds that I was driving and had drunk my limit. But there was one senior officer of that time who would twist your arm and tell you where the drink-drive patrols were operating that night so you could avoid them on the way home! Before any self-righteous reader takes issue, this was the 1970s. It was a different time and police attitudes simply reflected the misguided behaviour of people like me and certainly many of my colleagues.

I'm not proud to recall that I would regularly drive when over the limit and would sometimes rely on connections to get me out of trouble. On one occasion, when driving in the early hours from Sheffield to my parents' home in Chesterfield, I was pulled in by a patrol car that had evidently been trailing me for some time but appeared out of nowhere in my rear view mirror. 'It's a fair cop' were the exact words that came to mind as I climbed out of the car knowing I was well over the limit.

They asked if I'd had a drink, which I admitted. And then, instead of producing the dreaded breathalyser bag (which I'm ashamed to say I had used previously amid several close shaves), they merely asked me where I lived and how far I had to go. I told them a couple of miles and feared the worst. 'OK then, just take care on your way home,' came the reply. I still thought I was dreaming when I bumped into a mate from the force the following day.

Without me saying a word, he said: 'You were pulled in last night, weren't you?'

I said: 'How do you know?' A smile spread across his face. 'I was in the radio room when they called in with your registration number before stopping you. I saw it was you and asked them to let you off!' Let me tell you a few free pints changed hands after that— and it was worth every penny.

You may feel at this point that I was something of a juvenile delinquent. In fact, I was quite shy and reserved. Really. And I still am. It's taken journalism to pull me out of my shell from quite a sheltered upbringing which began in rural Kent. And the pub culture I embraced at work in the 1970s was just another part of that process. People lived and worked differently, not necessarily for the better. Attitudes were different, too. One example is that I know (from hazy recollection) that I made a Sheffield Cablevision appearance when completely incapacitated at Christmas 1974—

having failed to appreciate the extent of my inebriation until my slot began and I realised I was almost incapable of reading the script. Nothing was said! Not by manager John Brand who, by way of explanation, was pretty merry himself. And not by a single viewer apparently (although maybe that proves there weren't any!)

The point, though, is that this sort of excess was considered somehow excusable. Nevertheless, a good job I changed my ways . . . but not until after another example of the kind of working practice that would get you the sack nowadays. Radio Hallam's managing director, Bill MacDonald, was an exception to the general rule in that he frowned on drinking and banned alcohol from the building, which was extremely uncommon at that time. But he had some world-class boozers on his staff (Moffat, Moran and a rough diamond local DJ called Ray Stuart to name but three) and he had no control over out-of-hours activities. They were interlinked, of course. There were times when I had to start off programmes for Johnny and Ray while they slept off the previous night's excesses. Not that I should talk. One morning I was throwing up when I should have been reading the six o'clock news.

But my worst transgression—somehow unpunished—came in impromptu fashion when I turned up for a Saturday evening news shift, relieving a chap called Paul Reizin. Paul said he was dropping into the Dove and Rainbow pub just round the corner. Did I fancy joining him for a quick one after I'd read the six o'clock news? Things were quiet on the news front, as Saturday nights usually were, and I duly joined Paul after the news at six . . . and seven . . . eight . . . nine, 10 and 11. In fact, I spent virtually the entire shift in the pub, only departing just before each hour to sprint upstairs to scramble together and deliver bulletins that became increasingly incoherent as the evening progressed. Yet no-one seemed to notice, or at least nothing was said.

At other times you were so much under the cosh you needed a couple of extra heads and a dozen pairs of hands and feet. I can't remember a period of more sustained intensity than during the terrible winter of 1977–78 when I was Hallam's morning editor. Just getting to work from my home in Chesterfield 12 miles away was difficult enough considering the gritters were on strike and people were advised not to undertake any journey unless absolutely necessary. The one good thing is that at five o'clock in the morning I had the roads virtually to myself. Even then it was seat-of-the-pants stuff and I had to lean on the daredevil spirit of my erstwhile journalism lecturer at Sheffield's Richmond College, Ron Eyley, who, against my better judgment, had somehow persuaded me to do a parachute jump. Incidentally, the *Cessna* I jumped from was piloted by one James 'Ginger' Lacey, a Second World War fighter ace. So I also had to keep my weather ordeal in clear perspective!

Anyway, I thought of Ron as one morning I ploughed through up to a foot of fresh-fallen snow to reach the A61 Unstone-Dronfield bypass, a dual carriageway which was my usual route into Sheffield. It had a barrier partway across the entrance saying it was closed. It seemed to me that the alternative of the old road through Dronfield would be even more precarious—so I ignored the sign and went for it, just managing to crest the summit at the midway point while knowing that I had little hope of rescue (no mobiles in those days) or sympathy if I failed to make it. On reaching work, I announced on the first news bulletin that 'the Unstone-Dronfield bypass is closed'. I felt like adding the rider that people should ignore the single line of tyre tracks, but thought better of it!

3

NO FLIES ON THIS REPORTER

The 1970s were cavalier times in the media, a galaxy away from my latter day working practices (I hasten to assure the BBC and the several national newspapers who have enlisted my services). But the characters I have met, and still do, in the world of sport are much richer by comparison . . .

Take Len Ashurst. In the mid-1970s I wished somebody had! Hardman Ashurst was hired by Sheffield Wednesday to lick their players into shape and he was a fearsome figure for journalists as well, particularly for one wet-behind-the-ears 20-year-old learning the ropes on local radio. But Len also had a vicious sense of humour—as I learned to my cost.

After a game, reporters would pile into his small office and the session would be led by one-to-one radio interviews, which was pretty daunting in that Len would sometimes play to the gallery of newspaper scribes at the back. Following one game, a 1–1 draw if I recall, I started with what I thought was the safe question of whether it was a fair result. 'The only thing I've got to say to you Alan,' said Len sternly, 'is that your flies are open . . .' Cue an explosion of mirth as I made the classic mistake of actually looking.

On another occasion, I turned up on a Friday for a pre-match interview to be told Ashurst was waiting in the gym. He ushered me in and pointed me to an olden wooden chair placed opposite the desk. As I pulled it out, the chair just disintegrated. Len and his equally mischievous fitness trainer, Tony Toms, also fell apart.

What I failed to realise at the time is that, besides taking the proverbial, this was probably Len's way of being friendly. In the same way, he had a nickname for me based on Wednesday's slim midfielder of the time, Phil Henson, who was known as 'the flying chip'. Your even skinnier reporter was christened 'the flying crisp'. Ashurst was sacked a year or so later without too many tears from me. But I had a chance meeting with him quite recently and found him to be a very kindly pensioner! We happened to be sitting next to each other at a League Managers Association annual awards dinner. Len chortled at the fear he struck in me. Funny how age changes your perspective.

Len comes from Liverpool, which explains a lot about his sharp, caustic sense of humour. I had an even more embarrassing experience at the hand (literally) of Scouse comics before the 1979 FA Cup semi-final at Hillsborough between Liverpool and Arsenal. Stuart Linnell, who was presenting our show from a box at the ground, detailed me to do roving interviews with a radio microphone on the pitch. Besides being on the radio, these were tannoyed live to fans at the stadium because Hallam's programme used to be relayed on the public address system before a game. This was a heady experience for me as I chatted with, among others, Liverpool's legendary manager Bill Shankly.

Feeling more confident by the minute, I decided to try something different when I pulled up alongside Liverpool's goalkeeper, Ray Clemence, in the centre of the pitch. I did the interview with him on the stroll as we moved towards the end where his club's fans were massed. As we entered the penalty area, I went for the big introduction to spark the hoped-for explosion of noise . . . 'Liverpool fans, your goalkeeper . . . Mr Ray Clemence . . . ' Silence, total silence, greeted my announcement. Instead, they responded, in unison, with a wave of two-finger salutes. And these weren't aimed at Clemence, by the way! I was momentarily speechless because, of course, I could hardly describe the spectacle in front of me. Clemence just grinned; he'd probably seen it coming. Looking back, I doubt whether any other set of fans in the country would have reacted in that manner. In a strange sort of way, I admired them for it. It was clever and, more impressive still, it seemed to be a telepathic put-down from people whose sharp wit is on the same wavelength. But I can't say I appreciated it too much at the time.

Around this period, I had a first hilarious exchange with the famous cricket umpire, Dickie Bird. This was at the Queen's Park Ground in Chesterfield where I would regularly cover Derbyshire matches for Hallam. I should explain that our broadcast position was right among the players themselves on the pavilion balcony. One day, I arrived earlier than usual to set up my gear to find a flustered Dickie brandishing a broom handle. He was trying to push round the hands of the big clock which was on the pavilion wall above where I sat. Rounding on me, he remonstrated wildly about the clock being wrong and what was I going to do about it. Maybe I looked like some sort of handyman, I don't know, but it took me a little time to persuade this eccentric Yorkshireman that I had nothing to do with the club and was there simply to report the game.

In the years that followed, I enjoyed many much more convivial chats with Dickie. What a wonderful character. No novelist could make him up. I found him to be a man who is unfailingly helpful and has great generosity of spirit. But, of course, his frugal nature is equally well known. Following one interview for the short-lived *Today* newspaper, Dickie phoned me in a flap. 'Ring me back, lad, will you,' he said, putting down his receiver as if it was on fire. I promptly returned the call to find that he was anxious about a very minor detail that took all of 10 seconds to explain. I think his phone bill would have stood it.

My wife, Lynne, long-suffering because she is not a great sports lover, was distinctly unamused one day about a call she took while I was out. 'It's Dickie Bird, Test match umpire,' said the abrupt voice, asking for me to call back.

On giving me the message, Lynne remarked: 'I felt like saying 'I know who you are, you silly man!' Glad she didn't. People like Dickie (not that I can think of any others) can be much misunderstood by those outside their circle. All of us sporting enthusiasts have a lunatic tendency to a greater or lesser degree because we are so obsessive. Dickie is just a cricket nut. Oh, and by the way, a very fine umpire.

This was an era of iconic figures in Yorkshire cricket and I'm privileged to say I met most of them. This was mainly due to a grand bloke called Leon Cox, a businessman who had strong links with the club. Leon would come up for a chat during a game and then casually say something like, 'Do you fancy an interview with GB?' This, of course, was a reference to his friend (rather than mine) Geoffrey Boycott. Or Sir Geoffrey, as he was known to his army of followers. Now let me tell you that to approach the Yorkshire dressing room in those days was the cricket reporter's equivalent of entering a war zone. You dare not knock, let alone enter.

The side had a lot of great players, some entering their twilight years, and all strong characters including younger ones like Arnie Sidebottom, Graham Stevenson and the late David Bairstow. Besides which, the club and, to some extent the dressing room, was torn apart by internal strife. But Leon would somehow emerge from this no-go area walking side by side with the great GB who would present himself for a coveted interview with yours truly. Spectators and colleagues would look on open-mouthed. My grateful thanks to Leon and also to a former Yorkshire committee member, Sid Fielden, who had a similar talent for making the impossible happen.

I have to say I had mixed experiences with the interviews themselves. A word out of place and you were for it. But I couldn't help but like Boycott. Boorish, difficult, stubborn and opinionated, yes. But also an honest, passionate man of great intelligence who offered powerful insights into the game. It's no surprise that he has become by far the best, most entertaining and illuminating pundit on the Test match circuit.

Of course, Geoff could be a pain in the backside at times. You expected no less. On one occasion, amid the promotion of one of his books, he called in to the Hallam studios for an in-depth interview. All was going swimmingly until I suggested that, having only once skippered his country, some of his comments came across as if he was frustrated not to be the captain. 'That's poppycock is that, Alan—absolute poppycock,' he fumed. But he didn't storm out, of course . . . not with a book to sell. With me suitably reproached, he articulated his argument very well, even if my suspicions remained. Actually, it was good radio.

Then there was the time, with another GB book out, when I went to interview him at a meeting of Wombwell Cricket Lovers Society where he was guest speaker. This happened to be at the height of the infighting, with Boycott at loggerheads with the Yorkshire team manager, Ray Illingworth, the ex-England captain who was for many years a member of Brian Close's great Tykes team. So it was that Boycs played silly buggers. He was very good at that.

If I wanted to interview him I had to 'get permission from Raymond Illingworth'. This was before mobile phones, remember. I crossed the road to find a telephone box and, after calling a colleague to extract Illingworth's home number from my contacts book at work, I dialled the Yorkshire team manager. I found Ray to be a likeable bloke, but he was not best pleased to be bothered in this way and I couldn't blame him. I could sense Boycott was the real source of his irritation and that he knew Geoff had scored a petty point by getting me to disturb him. 'Of course you can interview him about his book,' Ray snapped. In turn, Boycott was clearly taken aback that I had managed to get the necessary permission so quickly and he duly obliged.

Another interesting exchange came during a rather grand dinner at Sheffield's Cutlers Hall. Boycott was there as guest of honour and some journalist colleagues asked me whether he'd mind us quoting from his speech. I approached the great man with a polite request during the drinks reception. 'No,' he said firmly. 'It's a private function.' I relayed that to my fellow hacks with a passing reference to the fact that Boycott could be 'an awkward so-and-so at the best of times'. Later I was to feel terribly two-faced about this remark. To my astonishment, Boycott opened his speech by referring to the privacy of the function 'as I explained just now to my good friend Alan Biggs'. I didn't know whether to feel flattered or embarrassed.

Friends are people you call up to go for a pint and I'm not sure many people could do that with Geoffrey. Certainly not me. But there were times when he would phone me at work, to the amazement of newsroom colleagues, and also at home. One conversation was perhaps typical of him. He wanted to know whether I would attend a sort of surgery at which he was putting forward his ideas for reforming Yorkshire cricket. It just so happened that I was otherwise engaged. My niece Emma had just been born and we were going to the hospital for a first viewing of the bundle of joy. I thought this would melt even Geoffrey's heart. 'This meeting is much more important than that,' he chided. I like to think it was with a touch of irony, but I'm really not sure.

For all that, Boycott was and remains a hero of mine. For me, no century, however slow, was boring. It was fascinating watching a perfectionist at work and I was always disappointed when he was out. Though not as disappointed as him. Once I remember him being caught on 99. He trudged stone faced up the pavilion steps at Queen's Park, Chesterfield and the next sound was one of a bat being flung in fury across the dressing room.

Another hero was the great Freddie Trueman, even though I was too young to remember his peak years as England's finest fast bowler. Not only did I get to meet and interview him on more than one occasion—I actually went out socialising with him. This was courtesy, yet again, of Leon Cox. When Trueman popped in to Hallam to record a radio commercial Leon was in his entourage. So not only did I get to interview the great man but I ended up joining the two of them for lunch. Fred, I discovered, was partial to gin and tonic—in preference to a pint of beer, despite his iconic advert for the bitter that 'drives out the northern thirst'. He also came across as a much more genial and refined character than his stereotype image, hair flopping and snarling four letter insults at any batsman who dared to stand up to him. I'm sure Fred worked hard on the image. Not that he wasn't a ferociously hostile fast bowler; just that he really seemed to be a very different character off the field. A gentleman, in fact, and a real pleasure to meet.

Ray Illingworth, too, came across as essentially a calm character, very much in keeping with his unflappable reputation as a captain and high-class spin bowler. I got to know him a bit during his ill-fated time as Yorkshire manager. Whenever Yorkshire came to Queen's Park he would sit close to my broadcast position on the pavilion balcony. Illy was within earshot of my reports so I had to choose my words carefully, even if I was determined to be honest in my opinions because I knew that people like him would have had no respect for toadying.

But I'll never forget the pressure I felt one day when not only Illy, but also almost the entire Yorkshire team, were crowded around me as I delivered a summary of the day's play. They had come together to watch the rescue act of a lengthy last wicket stand after nine of them had been out, mostly to poor shots (which, of course, I felt it my duty to mention). There was a deathly silence as I spoke and I have never been more nervous doing a report. The silence continued after I'd finished, finally broken by Illingworth saying: 'Fair enough was that.'

That'll do for me . . . I've never been prouder than at that moment.

Whenever I went to report on cricket, I always drove to the ground with the proverbial song in my heart. What a way to earn a living, especially at Queen's Park which was not only close to my home in my early days but also one of the most picturesque arenas in the country. I'd often meet my dad, John, and brother, Graham, at lunchtime. Besides being a keen cricket fan, dad was interested in my work and a constant source of encouragement. So was my mum, Iris, even if she didn't quite share the enthusiasm of the rest of the family. Mum would make us laugh when cricket outstayed its welcome on television at home. 'I've had enough of Benno Richo for one day,' she'd say in mock reference to the great Australian player and commentator Richie Benaud.

But covering the game wasn't all sweetness and light. After a particularly wayward performance by the Derbyshire attack, I passed David Harrison, the club's rather brusque chief executive, on the stairs at tea. Stupidly I made some throwaway remark about how bad the bowling had been. David was clearly already fuming about just the same thing. He didn't need a comment like that from anyone. If looks could kill I wouldn't be here to write this. 'Just piss off,' he snapped, fixing me with a glare. The fact that he probably agreed with my remark was neither here nor there. I should have shown more sensitivity and I decided to take his anger on the chin. No more was said and David acted like nothing had happened. Wrong though I was, I still felt some sort of apology was in order.

Although David could be surly at times, his downbeat manner was more than outweighed by a couple of the Derbyshire committee men who were always close by on the balcony to make announcements between overs. Brian Holling and Les Hart were both real cricket-loving characters who always found some humour in the game—even if it was at my expense after some faux pas or other. And there were certainly some rich personalities in the press boxes of that area.

Counties would have a travelling troupe of writers. Hence Derbyshire games were presided over by the formidable quartet of Michael Carey (who became the cricket correspondent of the *Daily Telegraph*), Neil Hallam and Nigel Gardner (both local and national freelances) and Gerald Mortimer of the *Derby Evening Telegraph*. You had to be careful not to exhibit any pretensions to a deep cricketing knowledge with these sharp sages in attendance. I showed them respect, they returned it with tolerance! And after a suitable period of apprenticeship, we became friends.

You had to tread even more warily in the Yorkshire press box. Best to sit tight, listen and learn. There was an assortment of characters who would travel together, work together and drink together—not necessarily in that order! They were Martin Searby (a firebrand freelance who, for all his excesses, was an accomplished writer and broadcaster), John Callaghan (the phlegmatic correspondent of the *Yorkshire Evening Post*), David 'Plum' Warner (the relatively quiet and mild-mannered representative of the *Bradford Telegraph and Argus*) and David Hopps (known initially as the 'hapless Hopps' because of his junior status but later to become an esteemed writer who worked his way up from the *Yorkshire Post* to *The Guardian*).

Together, they were as thick as thieves. Many a practical joke was played on the unwary outsider. Yorkshire had a bowler called Chris Pickles. They managed to convince a visiting writer that he was the nephew of the famous one-time actor and radio presenter Wilfred Pickles. Not true, of course, but the bait was taken. Then there was their secret code for recording statistics. You'd hear references to an innings containing 12 'Js' and two 'Ts'. Roughly translated, this was 12 fours (with the J standing for the cliché of 'juicy') and two sixes (often referred to as 'towering'). Occasionally, during a game at Headingley, one of the Yorkshire corps would casually ask: 'Any TGs today?' A colleague would check his notes and reply: 'Yes, we've had three.' You'd sit there wondering what vital piece of information you had missed—but you wouldn't want to betray your ignorance by querying something they clearly regarded as an obvious fact. It turned out that it was merely a reference to the number of jets passing overhead to and from the nearby Leeds-Bradford airport. Why TGs? It stands for 'thousands gasped!'

In such a way, the Yorkshire press pack would entertain themselves and others through even the dullest day's cricket. Their favourite code, and one I eventually cracked without asking, would be a question floated casually to colleagues after the first wicket of an innings had fallen. 'Is it nine, Plum?' John Callaghan would ask.

Plum would ponder the enquiry as if a difficult problem had been set and finally come back with 'Yes, I think it is nine'.

And someone else would back him up—perhaps the late Rob Mills, a pipe-smoking character who joined the *Yorkshire Post* after Hopps hit the national scene—by saying: 'Yes, I can confirm it is nine.'

I would sit quiet, simply hoping that this wasn't a crucial point. The routine was played out on many an occasion before the simple truth finally dawned. It was merely a reference to the number of wickets left in the innings! But, of course, I played the game by keeping this secret from later newcomers to the Yorkshire press box.

Mixing with players was another joy in spite of the fact that, in the case of my radio reports from Queen's Park, it was either after they were out or just as they were waiting to go in. There would be a cool-down period after a batsman was dismissed and then he would invariably come to watch from the balcony, sometimes to hear from me about his own dismissal! I'd then get to hear his rather more informed, though occasionally embroidered, version of events. Derbyshire's New Zealand Test opener John Wright was among the most gregarious characters I came across—especially if the conversation turned to gambling.

Around this time I came to form a close relationship with Geoff Miller, Derbyshire's England all-rounder, who I'd known from his earliest days with the county. For many years Geoff had a monkey on his back in that he'd never scored a first-class century despite getting into the nineties a couple of times for England—including once being dismissed for 98 against India at Old Trafford. How fitting that it was at the same ground that he finally cracked three figures with a ton against Lancashire in the county championship. I lived out the last 24 runs by 'watching' them on Ceefax at Hallam's studios in Sheffield. Seeing that he was 76 not out, I watched every flicker of the screen with my heart in my mouth . . . before ringing the ground to record a congratulatory interview at lunchtime. Geoff is now England's sole selector and is good enough to chat to me for the *Sheffield Telegraph* occasionally.

One unforgettable encounter of the late 1970s was with pop and rock legend Rick Wakeman. Well, two encounters to be precise. Wakeman's interest in football—he was a director of Brentford at the time—was reason enough for me to interview him during his visit to the station. Somehow I then got invited out for a 'lunchtime drink' with Rick and deejay Johnny Moran, who were old friends. That session took place at the Grosvenor House Hotel but I have no recall of when or how it finished—because I was under the table for most of the time.

But I do remember meeting Rick again outside the Bramall Lane ground a day or two later where, by happy coincidence, his beloved Brentford were playing. He's a very easy-going, unassuming sort of bloke and there was nothing awkward or forced in the way we renewed acquaintance outside the main entrance. It was just as well for him, actually. Sheffield United had a real jobsworth on the door, dressed in full commissionaire's regalia. By contrast, Rick was outlandishly attired as befitting of a star in the music business. But, of course, Mr Jobsworth didn't recognise him and, furthermore, was frankly insultingly incredulous as he refused to accept that Wakeman was a director of Brentford FC. But the commissionaire had come to acknowledge yours truly—albeit grudgingly at first—and I was able to persuade him that Rick was indeed who he said he was.

4

DREAM ON . . .

Becoming Radio Hallam's sports editor was the proverbial dream come true. I was just 24. That wouldn't be considered young at that level by today's standards but in 1980 I was well ahead of the game. Stuart Linnell had been offered a programme controller's position in the Midlands, where he has remained a big wheel in broadcasting circles, and I'm not ashamed to say I was so hot for his job that I could have pushed him out of the door. There were anxious times as he prevaricated a little but eventually Stuart agreed to join his old Hallam colleague, Ian Rufus, at Mercia Sound in Coventry. Hallam's incoming news editor, Jim Greensmith, kept me in suspense for a couple of weeks, but that just made the appointment all the sweeter.

Besides the extra responsibility, with management duty for handling the sports' budget and presenting three shows a week, the major change was that I became largely studio bound after four or five years of being out at events. There were times when they should have locked the door and thrown away the key.

One such occasion was an interview with Sheffield's British and European boxing champion Herol 'Bomber' Graham. Herol was a lovely laid-back character outside the ring (and sometimes even inside it as he had a classical style). And it's really just as well. I should explain that he was the first of a number of brilliant black boxers groomed by trainer Brendan Ingle at his stable in the under-privileged east side of the city. But I can honestly say I had never even considered the colour of Herol's skin, which is my excuse in advance for the absent-minded but shameful comment I made to him during a (thankfully) recorded pre-fight interview. It was only on playback for editing that I heard myself asking: 'Do you think your next opponent could be the nigger in the woodpile?' Yes, I can tell you are shocked. I'm still appalled about it myself and dread to think of the consequences of asking such a question today.

At the time, I was unaware of saying anything offensive or politically incorrect, having been on automatic pilot. The offending phrase must have been something that crept into my vocabulary as a youth during what was a very different age. To coin another phrase, it was just a way of asking if there would be 'a spanner in the works'. I remember Herol's reaction. He just paused and smiled before answering the question in the spirit of the meaning intended. Unthinkingly, I puzzled at the time over the curl of the lips . . . until I replayed the tape to hear in horror the wording of my question.

Somehow Herol handled it with dignity and humour, which was typical of the man. Thank goodness! I subsequently apologised, of course, and again he laughed. I like to think that the fact such a set of words appeared unprompted in my mind shows that I didn't consider Herol different, in any way, to anyone else. An episode that could have spelled a premature end to my career had somehow been successfully negotiated. Never to be repeated, I might add.

Boxing had to be an addition to my reporting and commentating repertoire—thanks to Herol's success. And it was courtesy of a local entrepreneur called Mike Watterson that I extended it further. Mike was the guy who had the vision to bring world snooker to the Crucible Theatre in Sheffield where it has remained ever since. As a result, a snooker rulebook suddenly appeared on the Hallam sports desk. This was during Stuart Linnell's reign but for reasons that became obvious when I took the chair, I ended up covering a lot of sessions on his behalf. We had a sound booth up in the gods which happened to be level with the dividing screen between tables—so that we could see both games simultaneously. I literally didn't know where to look and, considering my unfamiliarity with the green baize game, my head would be spinning.

Some of my reports were so vague that Roger Moffat took me to task, sending me up good and proper in a typical on-air rant lasting some five minutes. 'Mr Biggs, if you don't know anything about snooker then shut up and get out of it,' he said. And to think we were supposed to be on the same side. Funnily enough, I never minded about that sort of thing. It was always an honour to be the butt of Roger's acerbic humour. As far as I was concerned, publicity like that was worth having.

Fortunately, Mike Watterson and the players were far more tolerant of my ignorance. Together, they made a concerted effort to project the sport which, in the first year at the Crucible in 1977, was being televised for the first time. The one exception—perhaps you might not be surprised to learn—was the late great Alex 'Hurricane' Higgins, the biggest box office draw in this new sporting phenomenon and who sadly died in 2010.

The Irishman was, to put it mildly, a mercurial character. I received the necessary introductions for an interview and he agreed. But this first meeting was a disaster. I was operating a radio mike and it so happened that our engineers couldn't get a signal from the room we were in, where Alex was ready and waiting. All we needed to do was step into the corridor outside to 'remove' the wall that was blocking transmission. But Alex just threw a fit, refused my simple request and stormed off. He was a volatile character who would blow hot and cold. On a later occasion, I was invited to a snooker club where he was practising between rounds. He couldn't have been more agreeable and we could have talked all night.

All the other snooker stars—as they were to become in a big way—would co-operate right on cue. John Spencer, the first winner at the Crucible, even scaled a precarious vertical ladder to join me in our box for a chat after the final. The rest of the time, players would be marched post-match to our interview room by helpful tournament officials like Ken Smith, whose son Trevor is a respected sports photographer. And the players were unfailingly co-operative. What a different world from football where so much time is wasted waiting for interviewees who then don't want to talk.

For instance, Cliff Thorburn is a lovely bloke. Astonishingly, there was only one practice table at the Crucible in those days and, seeing it unoccupied one day, Stuart Linnell and myself decided we'd try to put into practice some of what we'd learned. Then Cliff came in to prepare for his next game and we immediately offered to withdraw. He would hear none of it and asked us to continue! I guess he thought that would be more entertaining. A few shots later, we did make our exit and could not be persuaded otherwise, so acute was our sense of embarrassment.

These were relaxed times. I recall interviewing Dennis Taylor in his dressing room *during* his first world final. Steve Davis would gladly stroll the city centre streets to appear in the Hallam studio. Steve was poker-faced at the table and was considered dull by the snooker public in those days (long before he became 'interesting'). I found him to have a great sense of fun. He enjoyed having a dig at my moustache, which I have to admit was akin to a caterpillar crawling across my upper lip. Other likeable personalities of that era included Terry Griffiths (who I interviewed after his 1979 win) Ray Reardon, Willie Thorne, Kirk Stevens and, of course, Jimmy White, who interrupted one of our interviews to wave to his many female fans crowding on a pavement outside the window.

One unforgettable moment—for the wrong reasons—did not involve the snooker itself. This was the time when it was under the banner of the Embassy World Professional Championship, sponsored by the cigarette company. I mention that because the 1980 tournament coincided with a rather more serious event—involving another kind of embassy—that has come to be known as the Iranian Embassy Siege. We broadcast live coverage of the SAS storming the building to release hostages during an extended

Hallam news bulletin which contained no other news content. However, we were contracted to include a snooker update in every bulletin under the terms of a sponsorship agreement.

So it was that after about 10 minutes of life-and-death drama, I was cued to with the words: 'And now snooker. With the latest on the Embassy World Professional Championship, here's Alan Biggs.'

If I could have been anywhere else at that moment I would have been. It seemed ridiculous and disrespectful (even laughable, as I sometimes chuckle when thinking about how this could have been a black comedy sketch) to take a report on people hitting balls into bags with wooden sticks on the back of something so profoundly serious.

I tried to sound low-key to the point of being a mumble in the background. But for me, worse was to follow. By far the most agonising spell of my entire broadcast career was the 20 minutes that followed a newsflash during the Falklands War in 1982. Colleague Dean Pepall and myself were commentating on a local derby between Rotherham United and Sheffield Wednesday at Millmoor. Midway through the second half, I was suddenly told to hand back to the studio and newsreader Jayne Irving, later of *TV AM* fame, announced that HMS Sheffield had been hit by an exocet missile. There were no further details, but this was obviously a grave situation during which it later emerged that 20 crew members were killed. Jayne finished the newsflash by simply handing 'back to Alan Biggs at Millmoor'.

I was mentally frozen. It had been an exciting game—eventually it finished 2–2—but I remember nothing of the remainder. For us, it couldn't be a case of carrying on as if nothing had happened. We had to tone down the excitement of the match to keep things in perspective, while wondering if we should even be discussing it at all. Later, on returning to the studio after what had been a long day, I recall feeling utterly worthless as I watched the station's news team working feverishly on a story that was far more important than any I'd cover.

Even more so today, sport has an inflated importance in our lives. We should never lose sight of the fact that it is entertainment 'at the end of the day'. But you can't under-estimate the effect it has on people's lives and how their morale goes hand in hand with how their football team is doing. So eventually I forgave myself—as I had to again nine years later when feeling similarly inadequate after the Hillsborough disaster.

The closest I came to physical danger was learning how to master Hallam's Studio A where all the presenters had to operate the desk, old-fashioned turntables and all, on their own. I was all arms and legs in scrambling to reach adverts (stacked in cartridges) in time for their slots, cue up the next record and remember which faders to open. At first, what I was actually going to say by way of links was the furthest thing from my mind, as listeners may have realised. Bridget Whitaker, one of our engineers, would goad me by saying I'd 'never be as good as Stuart', whose technical excellence contributed to making him the consummate professional. One of the most satisfying experiences of my life was when Brid, who was always up front and honest with a heart of gold, admitted that I had passed the test.

Once I was familiar with 'driving the desk', which looked like the cockpit of an aircraft but was really no more taxing than handling a car, I discovered there was no feeling on earth like running your own show. For those hours—five on a Saturday afternoon—you *were* the station, you and you alone. There was an exotic feeling of power and influence which I have to admit went to my head on occasions. It would take my soon-to-be-wife, Lynne, to keep me grounded. She was long-suffering during our courtship, as she has remained ever since!

We met during the course of separate holidays in Romania where I was doing a travel feature. It turned out that Sheffield girl Lynne knew me from the radio but she made it clear at an early stage that she wasn't unduly impressed. This was despite me helping her back to her room after she had, let's say, overly enjoyed a night out with her friends. In fact, we only kept in touch because I'd promised to play her a record on the programme and she'd missed it, thinking *Sportacular* started at 2pm rather than an hour earlier. So Lynne phoned the station after the show to complain that I had broken my promise! She says she wouldn't have bothered ringing otherwise. I'm glad she tuned in too late because she hadn't been prepared to give me her phone number while on holiday. Now we started officially dating, although Saturday nights were a write-off.

I would promise to call for Lynne at about 7.30, after I'd prepared the next morning's sports desk, but I'd feel so exhausted and yet so high at the same time that I would first go out for a pint or several with my late colleague and good mate Graham Chatfield. You needed some light refreshment to come down. So I was usually good for nothing by the time I saw Lynne. She would then take issue with a mistake or two . . . sometimes, indeed, she would be spoilt for choice. But Lynne took the more level-headed approach that this was just a job and I really think she has kept me sane over the years, besides presenting me with three beautiful children, Ashley, Rosanna and Isabelle.

Another great bringer-down-to-earth was Hallam's redoubtable chief engineer, Derrick Connolly. Let me stress he was a great mate most of the time. If handled with care, Derrick would go out of his way to support you in whatever event you planned to cover. He was also very generous socially. But on the job he could be a timebomb with a very short fuse. Best to stand well clear on these occasions—like the time Derrick literally blew up in my face.

I'd inherited a Friday teatime sports phone-in from Stuart who, of course, handled all the technical requirements impeccably. These involved operating a delay tape with a four second loop. All this meant was that the 'live' phone-in programme was actually being transmitted four seconds later, so that any offensive language (from callers, I hasten to add) could be deleted. But I found the procedure involved, as instructed by Derrick, a little mind-boggling. You had to immediately hit a button which transmitted a four-second jingle (unheard by you) to fill in the deleted four-letter gap. Once the button was hit, you, the presenter, had to carry straight on with just a part-explanatory apology for having 'lost' the last caller.

Looking back on this now, it all seems simple enough. But then you never think it's going to happen to you, do you? And you never know how you are going to react. This particular caller lulled me into a false sense of security by starting with what sounded like a reasoned argument. Quite suddenly, he blurted that Sheffield United were 'a load of fucking shit'. I was shocked and I froze. Just did nothing. The words went out because all I did was cut the guy off, saying we could do without that sort of language. Indeed, we could have done without it. All I had to do was hit the button. I didn't.

At that moment, Derrick Connolly hit the roof. What made matters worse for him—and me—was that this was early in the programme and he had some time to wait for me to come off-air. I guess he was stewing for about 20 minutes. When the time came, Derrick was waiting in the corridor outside the studio. There was so much steam coming out of his ears that his glasses were misted up. I had to stand speechless in accepting the biggest rollocking I've ever had in my life. What was amazing, looking back, was that Derrick didn't swear. He seldom, if ever, did. But it was a fearsome tirade all the same and he ended with the warning that if it happened again, he would take me and the programme off the air. I won't argue now just as I couldn't take issue then. Derrick was right and shock therapy was needed. I duly hit the blip button on future occasions (too scared not to!), although it helped that Derrick increased the loop length to seven seconds just to be on the safe side in working with such an imbecile.

The ups and downs of broadcasting are such that less than 24 hours after this debacle, I was making my debut on the national airwaves—with the help of Derrick and fellow engineers like Mick Adams, Mick Sylvester and Phil Davies. Hillsborough staged a

Saturday morning Sheffield derby with Wednesday and United meeting in the League Cup. ITV asked me to do a live report into the *Saint and Greavsie* programme at lunchtime. Hallam's technical wizards arranged the hook-up and on the shout of 'go' (I never actually heard the link from Ian St John) I gave it my best 30 seconds. It was quite an adrenaline rush, which continued through the afternoon as I had to dash back from the ground to present *Sportacular*.

As the snazzy programme title may indicate, the show was—and had been since Stuart's slick days—a mix of sport and music, in that order. I remember thinking the combination was a little strange before I actually worked at the station but gradually it seemed the most natural thing in the world and the audience liked it. Well, to be precise, two audiences liked it. We managed to please sports fans with comprehensive coverage interspersed with snappy interviews of some three minutes in duration (around the length of a record) and at the same time hook wives, girlfriends and people with only a fringe interest in sport. The ratings would see us wipe the floor with the sport-only rival programme on BBC Radio Sheffield.

You have to remember that, at this time, live commentaries on local radio were a rarity. Rights fees tended to be prohibitive for regional stations and it was only on the biggest occasions that either station's management would fork out. Hallam was naturally the more commercially-minded and the bosses knew that only in extreme cases would a single event match the audience for a show that was all things to all men—and women. For instance, running live commentary on a bog standard Sheffield United away match, even in some far-flung place like Plymouth, would only guarantee you an audience of perhaps 20,000 regular Blades fans. In broadcasting this, you would be alienating fans of the other five teams in the area—and switching off the non-sports followers. Compare this with the fact that over 100,000 would regularly tune in to the programme. It was a no-brainer.

The year of 1983 was slightly exceptional in that we followed Sheffield Wednesday most of the way to the FA Cup semi-finals. For several ties, including the semi at Highbury, I presented *Sportacular* live from the venue. This would be a routine arrangement now but at the time it involved all manner of advance planning and technical challenges. Plus a lot of physical discomfort.

An even better example came the following season at the cramped Manor Ground at Oxford where the press box was behind glass. This was no good for us because we wanted to broadcast the atmosphere, so we acquired a couple of seats in the stand. Dean Pepall and myself sat in the crowd squeezed between home supporters while juggling broadcasting equipment and sheaths of paper on our laps.

Linking the programme, never mind the commentary, was a fully concentrated task considering adverts also had to be hit at scheduled times. The trick was to make it all sound like a piece of cake for the folks at home. Oxford was a nightmare but the programme ran amazingly smoothly and, bearing in mind the extreme difficulty, I look back on it more proudly than even the semi-final programme the previous season at Highbury where Wednesday were pipped by Jimmy Melia's Brighton. In fact, I still have a message from programme controller Keith Skues congratulating me on the Oxford show. Keith ended with: 'No doubt this memo will appear again as we get Securicor to sit in when we come to discuss your salary review!'

In fact, my salary was to drop! Neither of us could have guessed that within four months of that memo—in February, 1984—I would resign. A story for later.

5

FACE TO FACE WITH YOUR HEROES

The first time I encountered Jack Charlton was on an English beach in the glorious summer of 1966. The second was covering his appointment as Sheffield Wednesday manager in 1977. The first time I was an autograph-hunting kid; the second, a cub radio reporter. There was very little difference in the way I felt on either occasion . . . I was in absolute awe. But the marked difference second time around was that I had to talk to—and try to get to know—England's World Cup-winning centre-half. Getting the man to talk was never a problem, though I can't pretend I ever got to know him. He'd never remember my name for a start—although many a player under his charge would fall into the same category, such was his famed forgetfulness! But you didn't really need to know Jack in the personal sense. In reality, everybody knows him well enough. Because what you see is what you get.

Take that first encounter as the perfect example. Can you imagine any star footballer today holidaying in this country, let alone one who had just won football's ultimate prize? Even in 1966, I doubt if any of Jack's victorious team-mates holidayed in such a public fashion as he did. But this was typical of the down-to-earth nature of the man. And as someone who once cadged cigarettes off me on the Wednesday team coach, Jack may also have noted the extra cost of going abroad!

So it was that on Weymouth beach, Jack Charlton appeared magically on the sands in front of an 11-year-old boy on a seaside break with his family. This was just a couple of weeks after England had beaten West Germany 4–2 at Wembley, an event that has been my generation's great fortune and privilege to live through. It was just beyond belief to see this unmistakable cult figure sharing the same patch of sand. But there he was squatting on a towel with his wife and kids. They were enjoying a picnic at the time this particular kid nervously interrupted them with a request for an autograph. Jack duly signed with no complaint about being bothered. His presence seemed to have been undetected by a good many; either that or I was among few people not to keep a respectful distance in what were more restrained times.

Not that there was much decorum in our house when Jack's signature—scrawled in pencil, which is all I had to hand—was traced over by my younger brother Graham in an attempt to make it bolder! I've now forgiven him for what was a well-intentioned effort . . . but it's taken a few years.

My second association with Big Jack was a whole new ball game, of course. No autograph books on this occasion—not even to make good that prized exhibit. Just a microphone in hand for regular interviews on Hallam. These could be comical at times. I remember one which came straight after Jack had delivered a furious four-letter verdict to newspaper journalists on a particularly abject Wednesday performance (trusting to their undoubted discretion). When I followed up with a radio interview, Jack's mouth kept opening and closing with no words coming out. He was at a loss to replace the ones that expressed how he really felt. I had to laugh, albeit inwardly at the time.

On another occasion—my most memorable with Jack—I heard those words full force and directed at me. His Friday habit was to knock around with players in a games room at Hillsborough. It was here that he would hold court to journalists for a pre-match chat—

but only after he'd finished a game of snooker, darts or cards. This time it was snooker. Jack and star player Terry Curran were locked into a frame that was very keenly contested. Before going further, I should add that the pair of them had a love-hate relationship. Both were voluble characters given to being stubborn—alike in many ways.

In one previous interview discussing Terry, Jack had told me (on the tape for broadcast) that 'every time he opens his mouth his brains fall out'. I used it because it was great stuff, only to get a call from Jack's chief scout and trusted aide, John Harris—the former Sheffield United manager and a lovely man by the way—to reproach me for my lack of judgment. In truth, I'd have given a younger, inexperienced manager the benefit of discretion—but as far as I was concerned, Jack was big enough and ugly enough to look out for himself. Typically, he never complained about it himself.

But this time at the Friday snooker game with Curran was very different . . . eventually. I was peering over the edge of the table otherwise minding my own business when a row erupted over the rules and Jack stormed over to me. Pointing at my recorder, he said: 'Let's get this on tape. I say I can have a free shot and there's a fiver on it between us. Can you look into it and find out?' I said I could do because of my new-found connections with snooker at the Crucible. So Jack explained the argument on tape and stated his case before Terry did likewise.

When I finally drove back to the studio my thoughts were far from the pre-match interview I'd also recorded with Jack. I lined up world snooker promoter Mike Watterson to adjudicate live on the phone after I'd played the clips of Jack and Terry in our 2.30 sports desk. Mike's verdict: 'You've stuck your neck out too far on this one, Jack. You owe Terry a fiver.' I was somewhat foolishly delighted with myself—first, for answering the question and delivering the answer and second, for coming up with a very entertaining piece of radio. Looking back, I should have phoned

Hillsborough with the information first rather than assuming one of the guys had heard it. But they'd heard it alright—or should I say heard about it. It was a day or so later when John Moss, a Hallam news reporter who helped with sport, told me there was a rumour that Jack was furious. I still felt the whole thing had been harmless fun. What I should have factored in was that Jack had lost the bet! I doubt I'd have heard a murmur had it been the other way around.

As it was, I heard plenty when I finally plucked up the courage to make the necessary phone call. 'Are you the fella that came down on Friday?' Jack stormed.

'Er, yes,' were the only words I managed for what seemed like hours but was probably only about 30 seconds.

This was a man who never wasted time getting his point across. It was simply one of those occasions for holding the phone away from your ear. His point, to put it in slightly more polite terms, was that this was a private wager and I had no business making it public. Naturally, I apologised—profusely! There was a silence and then Jack said: 'Now what can I do for you?' I could not believe I was being invited to talk to him about the following night's league game and, with great relief, recorded an interview there and then.

Any journalist will tell you how much they respect and admire that sort of approach. We can all take and accept a rocket from time to time; it's part and parcel of our job in a very passionate environment. Where it rankles is when the offended manager or player bears a grudge, often over an unintended slight, an honest opinion or, as in this case, a misjudgement. But Jack went even higher up in my estimation that day. He had his say in no uncertain times and then he drew a line under it. That was truly big of him; a trait I have welcomed in many others. There were no further problems with Jack, although he was still a touch intimidating at times.

What I failed to suspect was that he really relished a bit of give and take. He wouldn't mind people coming back at him—providing he had the last word. Still, I didn't do so badly. There was one time sitting in his office when he proudly pointed to the drinks cabinet he'd just had installed. He was so chuffed he even poured us both a drink. That'll do for me.

Even so, I felt at Hallam that the best man to untap Jack's full potential was someone who knew him of old. So I enlisted the then *Daily Mirror* journalist Peter Cooper—a trusted colleague and friend throughout my career right up to his sad passing in 2010—to do the 'Jack Charlton talk-in', which was a weekly chewing-over of any number of football topics. We gave Jack a few quid which he would literally stuff into his back pocket—and which overstretched my budget. But we got full value with some fantastic stuff which was due in no small measure to the fact that, besides being a stylish and respected writer, Peter was also an accomplished broadcaster.

As it turned out, Big Jack was just one of six members of the England World Cup-winning team it has been my privilege to interview over the years. I met Bobby Moore (as a visiting player at the end of his career with Fulham), Alan Ball (when managing Portsmouth), Gordon Banks (on a visit to his home town of Chesterfield) and Martin Peters (who dropped on my doorstep as manager of Sheffield United). But that's only five.

The sixth was Jack's younger brother Bobby Charlton. I first interviewed 'Our Kid' while he was on a tour promoting his football coaching schools. What followed was an invitation to sample the course first-hand by joining in and make a feature item of it. So it was that fellow Hallam presenter Dave Kilner and myself turned up on a football field at Wilmslow in Cheshire for special coaching from one of England's finest. Both of us were still young enough to have been playing the game at some level. Bobby (later Sir Bobby) obviously declined to make any influential recommendations . . . because our careers playing only charity matches carried on uninterrupted!

But what an experience—particularly being coached in striking a shot from distance by the master of the art. An abiding memory for me is Charlton's 25-yard rocket against Mexico in 1966 that effectively launched England's victorious campaign. We had been held 0–0 by Uruguay in the opening match and were toiling without success in the second game when Bobby suddenly let fly into the top corner. Having never attempted to score from such distance in any sort of game (six yards was more my range), I was fascinated to discover how difficult a technical skill it is to keep the ball down.

Charlton kept lining up practice shots from outside the area, telling me to hit them as hard as I could. Each and every one of them cleared the crossbar, however much I tried to keep over the ball. So I now look back with even greater wonder at that Mexico goal and the many others from Bobby's dazzling collection. And what impressed me just as much was his characteristic decency in somehow managing to keep a straight face. Had Bobby done his homework, he could have acted this even better. A couple of years before I had changed in the same dressing room as greats including himself and John Charles—on the same night but not at the same time. They were playing in a testimonial match at Rotherham United while we (Radio Hallam versus Radio Sheffield) were the six-a-side half-time entertainment for a crowd of over 6,000 at Millmoor. Quite clearly, Bobby declined to pass an eye over proceedings during the break.

One particular meeting with Martin Peters—who scored England's often overlooked second goal in the '66 final—was an equally inauspicious occasion. Martin, newly appointed as Sheffield United's manager, came across as a quiet, self-effacing sort of guy. Thankfully, too, he had a dry sense of humour. I remember turning up in his office at Bramall Lane and plonking my tape recorder on his desk. He leaned forward to begin the interview and was clearly puzzled by my sudden panic. I had forgotten to bring a microphone! It's a bit like wearing your best suit minus the trousers. Fortunately, Martin was tickled by this and readily agreed to wait for me to race back to the studio for my somewhat essential piece of equipment.

6

ROWS AND REUNIONS . . . BILLY, EMLYN AND SERGEANT WILKO

The late Billy Bremner was among the big names it was my pleasure and privilege to rub shoulders with, though thankfully not in the literal sense. The former Leeds and Scotland firebrand was every bit as pent-up and passionate as a manager. Another with whom you got what it said on the tin.

Billy was full of mischief but he was also quite a complex character. I had cut my teeth with him as the relatively young boss of Doncaster Rovers. Later, when he was in charge at Leeds, I had moved on to freelance work and gained a private audience in his office at Elland Road for a newspaper interview. Billy was nothing but friendly and welcoming but I should have listened more closely when, at one point of the conversation, he said he was so tunnel-visioned on matchdays that his wife could walk down the corridor and he would walk straight past her.

By chance, I found myself cast as Mrs Bremner at a Leeds home game just two days later. These were days when journalists often made their own arrangements for post-match interviews and weren't corralled by press officers. Not knowing if there were any no-go areas (other than the dressing rooms) at Elland Road, I wandered round a corridor to find Billy coming the other way. Yes, he walked straight past me. But then he stopped, doubled back and asked what I was doing there, pointing the way outside. It was as if we'd never met.

This was normal behaviour apparently and, as I was clearly out of bounds, I had no cause to be offended. Indeed, it became clear that he had forgotten the incident almost as soon as it had happened. And some years later, at a managers' dinner, Billy passed me a compliment that I shall treasure forever. He said he regularly heard me report games for Radio 5 Live and that I clearly knew my stuff. I was absolutely chuffed but also humbled by that.

Emlyn Hughes, a Bremner adversary during Liverpool-Leeds battles of the 1960s and 70s, was another larger-than-life character of that era. Emlyn was suddenly parachuted onto my patch when promotion-winning Ian Porterfield left Rotherham United to succeed Martin Peters down the road at Sheffield United in 1981. Besides being a household name as the former Liverpool and England captain, 'Crazy Horse' was also a star as one of the team captains on *A Question of Sport*. It seemed inconceivable that unglamorous Rotherham could make such a celebrity appointment, but then this was Hughes's first job as a manager and it should not be forgotten that Tommy Docherty once managed the Millers in the 1960s. All the same you wondered exactly who you were talking to . . . the wisecracking, impish and boyishly likeable housewives' favourite from the telly or the dynamic, ferociously determined player who wanted to transfer those qualities into management? A bit of both was the initial answer.

Emlyn was friendly enough but clearly intent on replacing a bit of the nice guy image with some of the nasty by conducting his interviews in businesslike style. And it didn't take much to upset him—as I was soon to discover. His Rotherham side had lost narrowly at Crystal Palace early in his reign. Gerry Somerton, our Rotherham reporter, had given his usual considered verdict in what seemed to me quite a sympathetic way. As sports editor, I made a routine call to Emlyn a few days later to arrange a time to pop down for the usual pre-match chat. He just exploded, telling me our report on the Palace game had been bang out of order and if we wanted to carry on like that we could sling our hooks. Or words to that effect. I was stunned but made a deal whereby I'd get the offending report laced up onto my tape recorder and come down to play it to him. I did so with a confidence that was reinforced when I heard again the inoffensive comments in Gerry's report. Not that he wouldn't have been entitled to criticise, as he correctly did on many occasions.

Emlyn joined me in leaning over a crush barrier behind the goal at Millmoor to hear the report played out. 'Nothing wrong with that,' he said. It seemed he'd got us confused with another radio station—or had been incorrectly told what was said. Emlyn would have been embarrassed at that point to hear another tape played out—of his rant down the phone at me! He put his apology into the form, on the spot, of a very good interview and I think he drew a lesson from the incident. But this is where reporters should, and generally do, follow the example of the many managers who, in a game full of rows, draw a line under a spat and swiftly move on.

Emlyn remained a willing and immensely good-natured contact through to his desperately premature death from a brain tumour in 2004. Once the new front of his management role was stripped away, he was exactly the bloke you saw on the box. I was invited to his home once to do an interview while he stretched out on the sofa and his wife stood doing the ironing. He got a lot of things right, did Emlyn!

Which reminds me of the most unusual venue in which I have ever conducted an interview . . . John Burridge's bedroom. 'Budgie'—a goalkeeper as eccentric as they come and who played for no fewer than 29 clubs—was in the bed at the time. His wife had answered the door and promptly invited me upstairs! This, evidently, was Budgie's routine every day after training during his time at Sheffield United—and everywhere else, for all I know.

When it came once to an impromptu invitation to the home of the late Ian Porterfield, another great bloke and a tremendous help to me, the front room was more than eventful enough. I was only there because I'd missed seeing him at the ground and he was good enough to say I could pop round for five minutes. This somehow turned into hours. Ian kept offering cans of lager; he just wanted to keep talking football. It was this warm-hearted enthusiasm that made him a success at Sheffield United, just as he had been at Rotherham.

I'll never forget, either, seeing how much it all meant to him after United had scraped a second promotion in 1983 on their way back from the uncharted depths of the then Divison Four. Ian staged a party in his office and invited all and sundry. When I walked in just after lunch, he jumped up and threw his arms around me. My last view of him that day was of him slumped across his desk. He was certainly tired and not the only one who was emotional! We were to feel the same way again when Porter, the legendary matchwinner for Sunderland in their 1973 FA Cup final win over Leeds, died so prematurely.

Howard Wilkinson, by contrast, can seem an icy character. I sort of knew him but didn't, if you know what I mean, when he was named Sheffield Wednesday boss in succession to Jack Charlton in 1983. We had worked occasionally together on radio match coverage with Howard, an FA coach working his way up via Boston United and later Notts County—to become a caretaker manager of England—in the role of expert summariser. Frankly, he was too pernickety and pedestrian to be punchy. But this meticulous attention to detail was to pay off hugely in management. Howard is reckoned to be dry, but he has a sharp sense of humour.

Early in his career, this was somewhat misplaced. At his Hillsborough unveiling, when someone referred to his background as a schoolteacher and asked him what he taught, he flatly replied: 'Children'. The assembled media did not see the funny side of what they perceived to be a clever dick put-down. Howard may not have intended it that way, but it left a clear impression. I was on the receiving end of something similar just as he was winning promotion to the top flight at the end of his first season. Another result meant Wednesday were effectively up without playing and I saw fit to use a home telephone number I had secretly squirreled away. Howard was intensely private but this was an occasion, I felt, when it was safe to ask him to step into the limelight. So I rang the number with the hope of recording a reaction to his triumph. I remember his exact words: 'Alan, I don't mind people having my home phone number — as long as they don't use it.'

That was typical Howard. Yet I had a liking for the man and I suspect the feeling was mutual. You could not help but admire his thorough managerial style and the results he produced, which later involved delivering the league championship to Leeds in 1992. Yes, the football could be rustic at times but he refined it at Elland Road. And yes, he continued to be difficult with the media, which proved a predictably shortsighted policy when he flopped spectacularly in his last job at Sunderland and people with long memories had their knives sharpened. It's only human nature for reporters to allow more latitude for people who have been co-operative.

Yet I have to say Howard was pretty good to me. He would be difficult to get hold of and would sometimes pretend to be his assistant, Mick Hennigan, by telling unwanted callers on his phone: 'Gaffer's gone for a run.' But he rewarded persistence and it was as if you were being put through some kind of test. I felt he allowed me a fair amount of access in the circumstances and he listened to reasonable requests. Coming across Howard at the time I did was ideal preparation for the next, much tougher phase of my career.

7

STRINGING ALONG

In August, 1984, I went back to my desk at Radio Hallam after a holiday in Tenerife and made a decision that wasn't anywhere inside my head when I drove to work. I resigned on the spot. Even my wife didn't know and she was rightly upset when I delivered the bombshell at home that night. I was suffering, as most of us do, from post-holiday blues. Combining that state with finding my desk looking as if a bomb had hit it, I wondered how on earth I was going to put together a two-hour programme in time for that Tuesday night.

Much as I had received and appreciated the help of news reporters like Tony Jones (a leading television commentator these days) and Duncan Rycroft (who became a big wheel in regional TV), I was essentially a one-man band. Most of the time, this motivated me and was a source of great satisfaction when the job was done at the end of the week. But making one more standing start after a fortnight of the good life was too much and I just snapped. I typed out a resignation letter there and then, explaining all my reasons. A newsroom journalist, Judy Laybourn, the only colleague present, looked on open-mouthed. I just didn't stop to think of the consequences. But I'm glad now of my impulsive behaviour because it proved—very fortunately—to be one of the best bad decisions I've ever made.

There had been a germ of an idea in my mind about going freelance and working for national newspapers because journalists like Mike Morgan and Peter Cooper were always encouraging me to sell stories from Hallam's output. Others on the patch, including Peter Ferguson and John Edwards, who both became esteemed writers for the *Daily Mail*, were equally accommodating. Mike, in particular, with his natural nose for a story, taught me a lot. With all their help, for which I remain truly grateful, I threw myself into a different role at the end of my three months' notice. Looking back, I couldn't have taken such a gamble if Lynne had not been in work as a teacher. She was our safety net as I rather self-indulgently tried to scrape together something approaching my previous income. Importantly, too, this was before we had children.

It was tough to start with and I fell short in the first 12 months but, in three years, I doubled my previous income as Hallam's sports editor and by a couple of years after that, I had trebled it. Further multiples have followed. But I hadn't made this move for the money. At Hallam, for instance, I hadn't even bothered to claim my expenses on some occasions. I was just too preoccupied with the job. That part of my character was to undergo a total makeover as a freelance, much to the gratification of my mum and dad who always nagged me—rightly—about throwing money away. But I found a buzz from story gathering and also from reporting matches for newspapers, which was a different challenge to radio work.

Howard Wilkinson was reasonably tolerant about my change of tack, even though I suspected he had even less time for scribes than broadcasters. 'Football needs good journalists,' he said, by way of a challenge. He allowed me a fair amount of latitude and even gave permission for me to join in pre-season training with the players one hot day in July. This wasn't an entirely straightforward request because Howard's gruelling training regimes were notorious and sometimes held against him by critics of his pragmatic playing style. Then again, as I've said, Howard had a sense of mischief and I'm sure he felt he might extract some enjoyment at my expense!

I reported to change with the players and join in all their drills, including some exercise routines that I found physically impossible. At one point, Howard rounded on me to recite several of his favourite homilies. He said he would ask me to trot them out at various times during the morning and woe betide me if I forgot. One of them has stuck to this day: 'Success is only a matter of luck. Ask any failure.' There followed a full-scale fast-moving practice game of two-touch which I was invited to join. Two touches was about all I mustered! 'Best player on the field,' said Howard wryly. His selection for the following weekend confirmed otherwise. Come lunchtime and after a sandwich in his office back at Hillsborough, Howard said his farewells. 'But you're back for the afternoon, aren't you?' I said.

'I'd like to do the full day if possible.'

'Very well,' said Howard. 'Think you can manage it?' He knew what I didn't. The afternoon in blazing hot sun was running, running and more running. Endless laps of the football field at Middlewood Road. But I managed to stay the course, albeit a little behind the rest, and I think Howard had a sneaking respect for me. When it came to putting together the piece in *Today* newspaper, at least, for once, I knew what I was talking about.

Howard helped me out with a few quite decent tales in return for playing ball with his stipulation that any interviews with players had to be approved in advance. So it was that one day I asked him for permission to talk to Carl Shutt, a snappy goal poacher who had forced his way into the squad. Sometimes you have a particular angle in mind but on this occasion there was no agenda; I just needed some sort of interview with someone from Sheffield Wednesday. By the way, I should add this was in an era when most of the nationals had offices in Manchester and produced regionalised sports pages. The Sheffield clubs were always heavily covered in the Yorkshire editions.

Carl Shutt took the call at home and the conversation was fairly low key. Suddenly he blurted out something that caught my immediate attention. He said he wanted to make clear that he hadn't been involved in a fight at the club. I hadn't heard anything of the sort but he said rumours were flying and he wanted to put the record straight. Foolishly, I obliged.

There were big headlines in three or four tabloids along the lines of 'Shutt denies Owls bust up'. I should have foreseen what would happen next. Instead, I happily calculated my prospective earnings, which would be quite considerable. Then I was taken aback to read Howard Wilkinson, in the *Sheffield Star*, slamming my 'wildly inaccurate and irresponsible reporting'. He was absolutely right and I can only say I must have been very naïve. Yet still I couldn't see anything much wrong at the time because there was nothing inaccurate in the reports nor any claim that a fight had actually taken place. But, of course, fans will think—and probably with some justification on occasions like this—that there is no smoke without fire. Had the rumours of a bust-up been more public, rather than mere hearsay volunteered by a player, there would have been some justification for the story. As it was, this was more of a non-story and yet one that aroused emotion. In that regard, Carl had also been foolish to volunteer it.

Naturally, Howard felt the reporter rather than the player should take the rap. He clearly suspected I had rung Carl with this specific question in mind. I hadn't. But Carl's version of events when asked for it by his furious manager was a different one. I didn't blame him for putting his spin on things, and still don't, but my integrity was also on the line. 'One of you is fucking lying,' was Howard's take on the situation. So I rang Carl and explained the pickle I was in while also saying that I didn't want him to take the rap. I was relieved and thankful when he admitted to his manager what really happened. Howard's apology to me was terse and mumbled under his breath, but it was there. While walking out of a subsequent press conference alongside him, he said under his breath: 'I guess I owe you an apology.' I accepted it and immediately offered him one by return for a bad judgment call.

I have found that it is not worth destroying professional and, in some cases, personal relationships for a story. You have to take the long term view as well as take a moral stand where possible. But I admit I have occasionally fallen short of this standard—particularly at the start of my career—because, in reality, behind every good story there is always some risk of collateral damage.

Here's another, which I don't regret because I was right, but which I could, and should, have handled differently. Ian Porterfield was under pressure at Sheffield United, wrongly in my view, because although they had started to struggle in the second tier, he should have been given the benefit of his two promotions. Someone inside Bramall Lane dumbfounded me by telling me Porterfield had been sacked already. A couple of further enquiries outside the club suggested Ian knew his fate and was just awaiting an official announcement. I jumped in quickly and had my first bylined backpage splash courtesy of *Today* newspaper, who had recruited me as a retained freelance.

It caused a stir and no-one denied it, but 48 hours elapsed before the news was confirmed. Needless to say, my stock with *Today* was very high. But the phone call I'd made in between times to Ian Porterfield had already taken the wind out of my sails. Not that he was angry. All he said was that he'd had loads of people in football ringing him to sympathise after reading my story . . . and yet he was still in a job as far as he knew. What Ian didn't say but had every reason to ask was why I hadn't rung him in advance of my story just to tip him off. I should have made that call considering all that he had previously done for me, but I had thought he knew what was coming. And I had angled the story very much his way, indicating how harsh it was for him to be sacked. But Ian deserved better and I like to think I learned from that exchange.

Who you should tell and when you should tell them is always a difficult call for a journalist in advance of an exclusive appearing. Above all, you don't want the story to come out before you have a chance to tell it. People in football talk all the time. That's how you come by your own stories, so others can get them by your own foolish gossip on occasions. This is by way of introduction to the two most spectacular rows of my career . . . so far.

8

NO HOLDS BARRED

The only surprise is that it took me until 1997—13 years after I turned freelance—to achieve the first of these conflagrations. Not bad going. Or maybe a sign that I wasn't doing the job properly, I don't know which. Although I had twice been barred (temporarily) by Sheffield United ahead of this time, that was mostly the result of petty politics and there was no real verbal exchange, more a cold stand-off. The circumstances surrounding the first full-blooded confrontation were so dramatic that the event has been chronicled elsewhere. Yet it all started with a bog standard transfer story.

The then Bradford City chairman, Geoffrey Richmond, had become a good contact dating back to his time at the helm of Scarborough. Many in the game, particularly managers, didn't like him because of his undoubted tendency to interfere. But my golden rule has always been to treat as I find and to try to avoid stepping into the crossfire of conflicts between people I know. There are times when this is unavoidable but it's best not to let the two ends meet the middle. In other words, use discretion.

So when Geoffrey tipped me the wink that Bradford were trying to bring back former hero John Hendrie from Barnsley, I saw only a decent story in front of me. With Yorkshire editions—sadly lamented by their absence now—still in vogue, I managed a measurable exclusive with the *Daily Mail*. It so happened that I knew and liked Bradford's manager, Chris Kamara, from his time as a player with Sheffield United. But it didn't occur to me that he might be opposed to the Hendrie deal or that

I should call him to tip him off about the story appearing. His chairman was an impeccable source, after all. Besides, I didn't want to stir any bad blood by going behind one contact's back to tell tales to another. Then there was the natural fear of the story getting out. Much as I know I could have trusted Chris, news has a way of snowballing when too many people are told 'in confidence'.

The day the story appeared, I went to Valley Parade for a night match between Bradford and Sunderland. Bradford lost 4–0 and I was not prepared for what happened next. 'Kammy', now a high-profile Sky pundit, has detailed his version in his autobiography, *Mr Unbelievable*. Memory plays tricks on all of us and there are some recollections that don't exactly coincide. So here's my account.

I was walking down a staircase after the game when I saw an understandably downcast Chris coming the other way. Here I agree with his account. 'There's no point going into my press conference,' he stormed. 'You're barred. If you want to know what's going on at this football club, you can ring that interfering busybody in there.' It dawned that this was a reference to Richmond and the Hendrie story but, as Chris says in his book, I 'played dumb'. I followed him up the stairs and the pair of us headed out into the now darkened main stand where he stated his grievance about me not ringing him and I stood my ground about having every entitlement to run a story I believed to be true. I said I had an impeccable source but refused to confirm Chris's suspicions about who this was, although I suppose it was fairly obvious.

At this point, Geoffrey Richmond himself appeared out of the darkness. This was as much a surprise to me as it was to Chris. It transpired Geoffrey had been alerted by his wife who had evidently witnessed the exchange on the stairs. I would have had no intention of bringing him into the row (contrary to Chris's suggestion that I was standing talking to the chairman as he came out of his press conference) and was prepared to play things down by understanding the manager's point of view (doubtless inflamed by his side's beating that night).

But Geoffrey weighed in with his booming voice. 'Alan, is there a problem?' he asked. I said there wasn't. 'Chris, is there a problem?' glowered Geoffrey, turning on his manager. Kamara said nothing so

Richmond followed up: 'Chris, this is a gentleman of the press and you will apologise to him.' There were mumblings from the pair of us with me apparently angering Chris even more by saying it didn't matter and I was sorry for any trouble.

As far as I was concerned, the three of us then went our separate ways. It was only later, and not at the time—as Kammy suggests—that Geoffrey threatened to sack Chris unless he said sorry. The story actually appeared in the *Daily Sport*—not that I saw it, honest!—the following morning. The next day, too, Chris did phone me at home and he did apologise. That escapes a mention in his book, but I can't forget it because the call came during Princess Diana's funeral which we were watching as a family. I took that call and accepted Chris's apology, fully understanding his point of view, without even knowing he had been threatened with the sack because I was unaware of the *Daily Sport's* story at that time (being an occasional viewer rather than a reader, if you see what I mean).

Happily, Chris and I always have a laugh about that row whenever we see each other and I'm glad he has no regrets about anything in his life, even though I was unwittingly a party to the souring of his relationship with Geoffrey Richmond. The axe duly fell later that season. As I have told Chris subsequently, it's ironic that my relationship with Richmond wobbled as a result of the sacking itself. I felt I knew Geoffrey well enough to be honest with him, as true friends should be, and I chanced a comment that I felt Chris had done a very good job and that I was surprised by the turn of events. He seemed bruised. 'Really, Alan?' he said. 'I thought we were friends.' Beneath the bluff exterior, Geoffrey appeared to have a surprisingly thin skin. But whatever anyone else says about him, he was very good for me and I am grateful.

In fact, close professional relationships are rarely to be confused with friendships. And I have found it wise to keep it that way, to maintain a discreet distance however well you get on with somebody. I am sure this applies even more the other way round! There are only a handful of people in football who I have been able truly to regard as friends and, even then, not in the sense of meeting regularly on a social basis. The respect and liking is always there, but going too far over the line can lead to distress because you never know how circumstances are going to conspire against you. Perhaps a better way of putting it is that you look to stay loyal to people who give you a fair deal. Keeping confidences is vital.

Another example of this delicate balancing act came close upon the Chris Kamara row. Come to think of it, that experience may have subconsciously affected the way I played this second bust-up. Again, it was an absolute bolt from the blue. Some people reckoned Danny Wilson had a sharp temper but I hadn't seen a trace of it. After a strangely uncommunicative spell when he seemed to take a vow of silence as a midfielder with Sheffield Wednesday, Wilson became a journalist's dream as boss of nearby Barnsley.

Not only did he earn huge credit for building the Barnsley side that was acclaimed by their fans as 'just like watching Brazil', and gave Oakwell a fairytale season in the Premier League, but Danny was also the perfect public relations man. He and I struck up such a close rapport that I helped him with third party approaches to a couple of transfer targets. Oddly enough, John Hendrie (then with Middlesbrough) was one of them and he signed for Barnsley. And when Danny moved on to take over from Ron Atkinson back at Hillsborough, he asked me to watch his back for him at his official unveiling. He was sensitive to accusations that he had somehow betrayed Barnsley, which he hadn't. I took care to ensure that the story was portrayed fairly to show that, in reality, his former club was in his debt.

Naturally, I was delighted that Danny was now at a bigger club in my area and therefore an even more important contact. Things began swimmingly. He confirmed the name of a rumoured goalkeeping target and told me he was flying out to Italy to vet him as a potential signing. I asked Wilson how that might affect Kevin Pressman, who was established as Wednesday's number one. He suggested it left Pressman fighting for his place, though I took this to be an off the record card-mark in the same bracket as the scouting trip.

I should now add that I had known Pressman for many years, longer than Danny, in fact. Possibly thinking back to the Kamara clash, I had a pang of conscience and decided to tip off Kevin the night before the story appeared. But I made a point of not telling him how another keeper signing might affect him. That is, I didn't relay Danny's remarks. In fact, it was normal for clubs to have two senior keepers and Wednesday only had one. All I said was that he would read in the morning about a possible bid for another keeper and that I wanted him to know in advance. But I stressed that he was not to tell anyone that I had phoned him; in effect, to save any response until he had seen the story.

A couple of days passed before I phoned Danny to follow up on his scouting trip. He was obviously waiting for the call and just exploded. 'I'm fucking furious with you,' he yelled. How dare I unsettle his goalkeeper was a polite translation of what followed. Knowing that Pressman must have said something—seemingly in advance of publication—I understood Danny's anger. I immediately admitted what I'd done and tried to explain why. But he was still seething and in no mood to listen.

Kevin then made matters even worse by publicly threatening to demand a move in the local paper, the *Sheffield Star*. It was news to me. Danny responded by refusing to talk to the paper for a spell, which was an overreaction, I felt. Rather than aggravate the situation by ringing Pressman, I ventured a call to Wilson and got short shrift. Danny clearly blamed me for the rift, saying that someone at the club had told him I was a troublemaker. He didn't give a name, though I later heard a rumour that the chairman, Dave Richards, had been quietly fingering me. Whether this was right or wrong, it would have explained a lot because my excellent relationship with Danny Wilson just disintegrated.

It just shows that when it comes to who to keep in the loop, you can't win either way. This became something of a 'domestic'—a temporary fall-out with your nearest and dearest. I felt I had done little wrong. Rather, I had been let down by someone I tried to help. So I wrote explaining everything to Danny, whose reaction I understood. I reminded him how I had done similar favours for him, stressed how much I valued our relationship and hoped he would see things differently. He did. 'I really appreciate you writing like this,' he said. 'Let's call it a draw.' I drew the same line with Kevin, one of those players who would always oblige with an interview. He—along with others of the era like Alan Kelly, Simon Tracey, Brian Gayle and Ritchie Humphreys—would gladly hand out prizes at my son's junior football awards. There is a lot of good done by footballers that escapes the headlines.

But Danny was never quite the same for the rest of his Hillsborough reign and I put that down to his stressful surroundings. Working for Sheffield Wednesday has done strange things to many of its managers over so many lean years. The burden is intense. I reckon even Danny might admit he lost the thread occasionally. It seems to happen to nearly every Owls manager. For instance, I found I was one of several reporters left in no doubt by 'sources close to' Wilson that he would try to shift Paolo Di Canio and Benito Carbone, the two gifted but temperamental Italians signed by his predecessor David Pleat—who himself admitted this was one too many! Careful speculation followed.

Then Wilson seemed to blow his own cover, calling some of his players 'Fancy Dans' in a furious outburst after a shock home defeat in the League Cup. Indeed, both Italians had pussyfooted around and this was fair game for interpretation by clued-up journalists. But the whole thing blew up in all our faces. Danny angrily denied he wanted to sell either player and blamed the media for the ensuing row.

By this stage I was a regular 5 Live match reporter and had to supervise a down-the-line interview between Wilson and the programme presenter—on the subject of the two disaffected Italians—before a home game with Arsenal. He was apparently so upset with me that not a word passed between us as I handed him the mike and the headphones and collected them from him afterwards. Danny took the opportunity to slam the media in that interview while standing alongside a target he simply couldn't miss!

We should now check the date. It was September 26th, 1998. That day Di Canio shook football to the core and provided me with the biggest matchday incident of my career. More of Di Canio's infamous shove on referee Paul Alcock in a later chapter. Suffice it to say, it was difficult, if not impossible, in these circumstances to fully close the rift with Danny at the time. But it takes two to create a stand-off and I was just as much to blame. There was a spell of months when we didn't speak at all.

That was largely self-imposed by me, rather childishly and partly to show that two could play at that game. During this awkward time, I made a point of reinforcing my original position by supporting Danny wherever possible—because I still believed in him as a manager. Then I approached him for a resumption of normal relations, which he readily agreed, though this was in the final throes of his ill-fated reign.

It has to be said that Wilson made some bad buys towards the end. But there was the whiff of broken promises from a weak board and he certainly didn't deserve the indignity of a group of Wednesday-supporting local MPs making a public call for him to be sacked. He was sore about that abuse of their position and rightly so.

On a personal level, I certainly learned from what happened during Danny's time at Hillsborough and perhaps he did likewise. It was about circumstances more than anything. I like the bloke and we've spoken since as if nothing had happened. Just as it should be. And I'm delighted he has had further success during spells with, among others, Bristol City, Hartlepool and Swindon. Wilson then returned to my patch across the city at Sheffield United—as the first ever to have managed both rival clubs—in May, 2011. He must also have become the first in the city's history to have faced a demonstration calling for his removal on his very first day! Actually, this couldn't have happened to a better bloke—because Danny is a tough cookie who won't have been the least bit fazed. He is also very honest and highly principled, a real pleasure to know. I should add that ongoing friction between managers and journalists isn't necessarily the norm. I have worked with almost 40 managers in Sheffield football and have got on with most of them. The fall-outs never lasted.

9

BIG RON, TRICKY TREVOR AND DAVE 'HARRY' BASSETT

A rare golden era for Sheffield football and, comfortably the most enjoyable of my career, lasted from early in 1988 to the end of the 1994–95 season. Happy days! Where there had been a grey drabness at both ends of the city, there was suddenly glorious technicolour. And I measure that in respect of the personalities as much as the two teams' considerable achievements on the field, which crystallized in the form of an all-Sheffield FA Cup semi-final in 1993.

A cockney bundle of energy called Dave 'Harry' Bassett bustled in at Bramall Lane and Big Ron ('Mr Bojangles') Atkinson then swaggered through the saloon doors at Hillsborough shortly afterwards. In terms of character, background and image they couldn't have been more different. But they both had style, charisma and a rich sense of humour. Both were also excellent at their job. In my time, I have seen no two Sheffield managers hit the scene with more personality and impact than these two. The fact that they were around in tandem, albeit for only a couple of years, made it a special time.

The bare detail of success on the field doesn't do this period full justice because it was so much about the richness of two well-defined personalities. Bassett suffered an early relegation he was appointed too late to avert and then hoisted the Blades into the top flight in two successive leaps, echoing his rags to riches story at Wimbledon. Even better, Sheffield United somehow stayed among the elite for four years. Wednesday, too, suffered an early drop under Atkinson. But the following season, they were back alongside the Blades with promotion topped off by landing the League Cup, the club's first trophy for 56 years. And it seems so hard to believe now that the Owls beat Manchester United in the final.

Big Ron's impact at Hillsborough was the most immediate and startling I have seen from any manager before or since. When he entered the building in February, 1989, the whole atmosphere of the place lifted. Wednesday had wavered in their ambition by allowing Wilkinson to defect for Yorkshire rivals Leeds United—'to better himself' according to the chairman's startling admission at the time. And his assistant, Peter Eustace, endured a torrid four month tenure. Eustace and I fell out during that pressurised time but no grudges were held and my major memory of Peter remains untarnished as a classy Wednesday midfielder of the 1960s.

He had been subject to the sort of austerity that saw an over-achieving side tail off under Wilkinson. Atkinson's emergency recruitment drive marked a startling change of direction. Although he was only contracted until the end of the season initially, Big Ron was a big-name boss in his prime, having managed West Bromwich, Manchester United and Atletico Madrid. Further, he was accustomed to having money to spend and promptly levered open Wednesday's coffers to sign Carlton Palmer for £750,000 from former club West Bromwich Albion.

What was even more impressive was that Ron made a charismatic impression despite what seemed to be a clear and conscious decision to modify his style. It's fair to say Ron was intensely image conscious and one of the most noticeable features of his first day was the complete absence of expensive jewellery. Only his personality sparkled. The job of saving the Owls from the drop was a serious business and he gave short shrift to a fanciful suggestion from me that Wednesday might one day become the vehicle to land him the league title that eluded him at Old Trafford. All that mattered was the next three months—and it mattered to him quite a lot when you considered what he stood to earn, as we'll discover shortly.

But Ron was friendly and engaging, seeming to strike an immediate rapport not only with the people around the club but also with the media, who he recognised (as some managers incredibly don't) as his link with supporters. What struck me most was that in a little first-day session with a handful of Yorkshire-based newspaper reporters he addressed us all by name. I was particularly impressed because, unlike some of my colleagues, I had never met him before. In truth, I had been a little apprehensive because he seemed a formidable character. But behind the front was a different persona, a touch egotistical and wanting to be the centre of attention, but also serious-minded and deeply thoughtful.

To my greater surprise, Ron gave us his telephone numbers (home and mobile) and said that if anyone wanted to pop down to the ground for a quick word, he was available most days at around one o'clock. On his second full day, I put this to the test. Right back Mel Sterland was being linked with a move to Glasgow Rangers. After just a few minutes' wait, I was ushered into Ron's office and he gave a straight answer to every question. I think he sensed that access had been tight for us in the past and wanted to make a good impression. Indeed, his Friday press conferences were more akin to a chat in a friend's front room over a cup of tea.

Not that Ron suffered fools gladly. Well, actually, in a way he did. There was a local radio reporter of the time who had a somewhat outlandish dress sense and who, more importantly, didn't seem to know a lot about football (which wasn't his field as a press-ganged news reporter anyway). He would have to interview Atkinson in front of the rest of us. Ron would play to the gallery, taking obvious delight in sending him up. I have to say I found it uncomfortable and not at all funny. There but by the grace of God go all of us . . . as I remembered from my days with Len Ashurst!

But, speaking as I found, Ron was brilliant to work with and I was even to emerge unscathed from a sticky incident quite early in his spell at Hillsborough. By chance, I discovered from a reliable source the actual amount Atkinson was being paid to keep Wednesday in the top division. Providing he kept them up, he would receive £90,000 for three months' work. This would go down as a pittance today but it was a staggering figure by Wednesday's standards at the time. On the day I was told this, I had already been in touch with Ron about a bid to sign Mitchell Thomas, the Spurs defender, who spent the afternoon in his office. Atkinson promised to keep me updated. My dilemma: Should I make the follow-up phone call without mentioning the big cash story which would be running next day? Or should I come clean?

I'm glad I took the latter course in the end. Not only was it morally the right thing to do, but I think Ron respected me for it on two counts. Firstly, that I fronted up and secondly that he couldn't scare me into dropping the story. But it was a difficult conversation, to say the least. Ron said I might be wrong with my figures. 'Are you sure?' was one of his favourite expressions. Cleverly, he didn't badger me much about where the information had come from—not that I would have told him, of course.

If he was irritated about a leak—as he must have been—he knew that to show it would have been tantamount to admitting the figures were correct. All he did was leave me in turmoil over whether to run a story he plainly didn't like. I took the risk of souring the relationship before it had even started and went ahead, fearing the consequences. There are times now when I admit to turning a blind eye to sensitive stuff on occasions, but a thrusting, young reporter could not ignore this calibre of story when he knew it to be true.

Ron Atkinson was terse when I next spoke to him on the phone but he quickly came round. I liked to feel at the time that a little mutual respect had been gained. Anyway, you hardly had to look outside of Ron for Sheffield Wednesday stories. His mind was so sharp that he knew the line he was going to throw out—even before you dropped your bait. He'd give routine answers to a few questions, enjoying the role play. Then he'd come out with a little nugget, either a brilliant quote or a genuine story, and wait for a second while it registered. Heads boring down into notebooks getting it all down would be his cue. A snap of the fingers and a beaming smile: 'There's your line,' he'd say. And he'd be right. None of us minded that we hadn't really needed to work for it. Then the pens would be put down and Ron would hold court privately on any number of topics, not necessarily football.

It helped that he had hands-on control of transfers, negotiating with clubs, agents and players. Ron would know exactly what stage a deal had reached and when it would be safe to tip you the wink. The one irritation was that he had a contract with *The Sun* and would give them the bigger ones while everyone else caught up. But this was beyond our control and in the main Atkinson was very good. If you found something out and put it to him, he wouldn't try to deny it. This contrasted with his second spell at Hillsborough in 1997 when, during another survival mission, he was required—as was becoming the custom—to keep out of transfer negotiations. Ron was a different man second time around, quite prickly even, but I prefer to think this was because he resented having his hands tied and we met again under happier circumstances shooting a video when he was managing Coventry City.

Many people have told me over the years that I have 'a good face for radio'. You won't be surprised to learn that Ron was the first. I would combine the day job with reporting Saturday and midweek games all over the place, mainly across the North and Midlands, for 5 Live. From remarks he made I could proudly count Atkinson among my occasional listeners, it seemed, and I have to admit it helped having two parallel careers. They would complement each other. I picked up enough kudos with Ron to become 'Biggsy', the nickname I have lived with since I first went to school. I didn't much like it then but whenever I hear it in my job it tends to be reassuring because I automatically know I must be doing something right.

Atkinson would indulge in private jokes with the press, often brilliantly disguised. Once, during a poor run of results, he opened in sombre fashion and said he was thinking of switching to a 4–4–3 formation. After a couple of seconds, I twigged but said nothing because my three colleagues were eagerly taking it all down. Ron just winked at me and proceeded to reel them in before the realisation dawned that you couldn't have 12 players (including the goalkeeper) on the field.

Another time, he staged a comical entrance for Trevor Francis, the former England striker he had just signed at the age of 36. Ron gathered us all in a reception room and had a compliant Francis carried in on a stretcher! The room collapsed in laughter and Trevor gleefully went along with the joke. But Ron was also at pains to point out that this was a private prank and he went to great lengths to ensure there was no photographer in the room.

Indeed, I'm sure that snappers, as we call them, had a very different view of Atkinson. He could present two contrasting personas, one bristly and businesslike and the other completely laid -back. Ron was in the latter mode as we completed a special series of features on his life that appeared in the *Daily Express* in 1991. All that remained after a lengthy interview in his office was for the paper's photographer to come in and take a picture.

Ron kept the snapper waiting and instead poured me a drink, which was the cue for an off-the-record chat about any number of things. He mentioned that he had given a bollocking that day to one of his best players, John Sheridan. But it was clearly carefully calculated. 'You need a bit of anger around the club,' he said. With the drinks finished Ron summoned the snapper into his office and immediately changed character. Clapping his hands to demand attention, he told the guy straight: 'Right, no trick shots, no cheap shots—let's get on with it.'

It seemed Ron could morph effortlessly from one to the other. In the build-up to Wednesday's League Cup final with Manchester United, the team lost 1–0 at Sunderland in what was actually a more important game because promotion was the essential prize being pursued that season. The previous year, manager and players had taken their eye off the ball with top-flight safety looking assured and were relegated with a crushing 3–0 home defeat to Nottingham Forest on the last day (while the neighbouring Blades were winning at Leicester to take the Owls' place in the old First Division). That sunny day, Ron's bright and cheerful yellow t-shirt was an absolute contradiction to the prevailing mood. He was furious and told his team—a very good one and far too good to go down, as they subsequently proved—that each and every one of them would be staying put to make amends.

Ron always behaved as the man for the moment. The following season was, indeed, an act of atonement and it provided a further example of the manager's psychological mastery. Going for promotion, Wednesday suffered the aforementioned irritating defeat at Sunderland in the build-up to that Wembley meeting with Manchester United in the League Cup. You can understand Atkinson was not best pleased because promotion was far and away the most important prize. The day after the Sunderland defeat came the scheduled Wembley press call and I imagined Ron would still be stewing after a late-night return from the North East and little sleep. Instead, he breezed in with a smile on his face, clapped his hands and shouted things like 'lovely jubbly' in imitation of Del Boy from *Only Fools and Horses*. This unnatural mood swing was a hallmark of his professionalism. It was probably forced but it was convincing at the same time.

Ron had a knack for creating the right atmosphere and knew that he had to generate a party feel in the approach to Wembley. Another masterstroke on the day itself was to hire his comedian friend, Stan Boardman, to do a spot of stand-up in the team coach on the way to the game. A relaxed Wednesday beat Ron's old team with a memorable goal from John Sheridan. I was among a handful of Yorkshire-based reporters invited to join the team for their celebration at the Royal Lancaster Hotel. Ron lived it up, taking the mike to belt out a few Frank Sinatra numbers.

We arranged to see him in the hotel next day for a follow-up interview. It was after lunch, as I recall, and training had consisted of a little jog round Hyde Park. Two days later, it was After the Lord Mayor's Show as the Owls were held 0–0 at home by Leicester. But something has to give in those circumstances and Ron lived by the motto of enjoying his successes to the full. He was right. Howard Wilkinson once admitted to me that one of his biggest regrets as a manager was dwelling too much on the failures and not allowing himself to indulge more in the good times. Besides, Atkinson's men duly clinched promotion.

I was such a confirmed admirer that I wrote him a thank you letter after he defected to Aston Villa that summer in somewhat disreputable circumstances. Ron was good enough to reply, saying I could look him up at Villa any time I wanted. The pull of Villa Park was understandable enough. They were Ron's team and he still lived on the southern fringes of Birmingham, which made the daily round trek to Sheffield such a gruelling bind that he actually looked ill during one part of his reign. But he still changed his mind twice about the Villa offer.

When Wednesday's chairman Dave Richards persuaded Ron to turn down the opening approach, Atkinson was wheeled into a Hillsborough press conference to say he just couldn't walk out on the team he had created. But you could tell his heart wasn't in the words and he was regretting passing up a dream. A week later, Ron did a U-turn and joined Villa anyway. That didn't stop Richards from calling for his services again after David Pleat was sacked in 1997. But this time, Richards dispensed with Atkinson once relegation was successfully avoided. Ron clearly felt he had been used and some suspected an act of revenge. But the old saying—

what goes around comes around—is undeniably true.

I have to admit I wasn't sorry to see Atkinson go on this occasion. He'd proved uncharacteristically prickly, probably because transfer negotiations were taken out of the hands of a man who loved to wheel and deal. But he's not a grudge-bearer. Ron was in fine form when I saw him quite recently at a game where he was working as a radio pundit. He couldn't resist showing off a watch he'd just bought in Dubai which, James Bond style, doubled as a mobile phone. 'Had to have it,' he said. 'No idea how it works, mind!'

On reflection, my relationship with Atkinson second time around at Wednesday wasn't helped by the fact that I'd formed a close relationship with his predecessor who I found to be one of football's gentlemen. 'Pleaty's pal,' was how Ron referred to me on one occasion. I found David to be a deeply conscientious character who agonised over every last detail in the job. He would rarely, if ever, talk about anything other than football and his consuming passion was always in danger of doing just that—swallowing him up.

There were times when David would appear indecisive because he would give every judgment almost too much thought. Nothing was ever simple with him and he was not a prolific provider of stories, partly because his thinking was so complex; issues were seldom black and white, nearly always a shade of grey. But I always felt he would genuinely try to help and a trust developed between us. He confided that he had to break up what he felt to be an ageing side. That was made more difficult by the fact that there were big, popular names in his dressing room like Chris Waddle, Des Walker, John Sheridan, David Hirst and Mark Bright. Strong characters most of them, as well.

You sensed that David struggled for authority in the dressing room, but he began to rebuild and achieved a high placing in his second season. A 6–1 hammering at Manchester United, combined with an expensive gamble on the two Italians Carbone and Di

Canio ('I should have settled for just one,' David later confided), finally finished him. I thought he deserved more time and support during what was an obvious transition period.

Not everyone was sorry about Pleat's departure, but I was personally sad to see him go. Among other things, he offered great advice and encouragement in my broadcasting career. As a radio pundit himself, David would listen intently and some of his comments were a terrific boost to my understanding of the game as well as my confidence. I'm delighted to have seen him continue as a skilled summariser who imparts knowledge in a perceptive way. We only ever had one minor argument and that ended with him sending a letter of apology, which was typical of the man.

This concerned Wednesday's Dutch winger Regi Blinker following a story in the *Daily Mail* that he was open to a move from Hillsborough. David rang me in a fury to say it was utter rubbish and that Regi would confirm as much. Considering my links with the paper, he asked — well, more demanded — that I phone Blinker to get him to put the record straight. When I did, Regi plainly didn't know how to respond. He said there was nothing wrong with the story; in other words, the rumours were true. I rang Pleat in a huff and told him that in no circumstances was he ever going to do that to me again, especially as I had no responsibility for the original story. Actually, I should have refused to make that call.

David, always a fair man, recognised my point and wrote something quite clever along the lines that as he got 'older and Owler' he realised that he could overreact at times. It's the first and last time I've ever had such an apology from a manager. Not that it was necessary because it was a minor altercation that had already been sorted. But it's a mark of Pleat's genuine humility as a person that he made a gesture I really appreciated.

The last time I saw David was when we both delivered eulogies at the funeral of Danny Bergara, the Uruguayan coach who became something of a pioneer in English football as a forerunner of the foreign influence. It has to be said that appointing Danny as coach at Hillsborough was perhaps David's biggest mistake—for both of them. Bergara was much misunderstood. His incredible fervour for football, combined with his often comical interpretation of the English language, made him appear an eccentric character. If he had been born here, I'm convinced the impression would have been markedly different and he would have gone much further than even the remarkable success he achieved with unfashionable Stockport County.

Danny had personally mastered all the skills and could demonstrate them. He could even take a coin out of his pocket, drop it, flick it up off the back of his foot and land it smack in the centre of his forehead. That party trick only added to some people's impression that he was more of a clown than a coach. But Danny, who first worked with David Pleat at Luton when both were coaches under Harry Haslam, deserved to be taken seriously. His final years were spent in frustrated exile from the game that shunned him and he died tragically early. But I only remember his smiling face and his impish humour because, like David, he was a great source of encouragement to me. And I was honoured when his wife, Jan, asked me to speak at the funeral.

Among a packed congregation that day was one Dave Bassett. He and Danny had different ideas when Bassett arrived to take charge of Sheffield United, where Bergara was coach. But changes of backroom staff are usually routine and rarely personal. There was no fall-out as far as I'm aware because Dave always treated people properly—his man-management was second to none—and it was typical of him to travel north from London to attend Danny's wake in Sheffield.

Dave 'Harry' Bassett hit a slowly suffocating Bramall Lane like the proverbial breath of fresh air—well, more a hurricane, to be precise. After a wild early stab at Lawrie McMenemy, I got the story in advance that Bassett was likely to be United's next manager. I had come across him a few times with Wimbledon and had formed the impression of a decent, open, fearlessly honest character who spoke his mind, albeit a bit of a rogue who could be accurately described as a rough diamond. What I had seen from a distance was exactly what I got when I obtained Bassett's home number and ran the United vacancy past him. 'Yes, it's a job I'd consider if they want me,' he said, refusing to disguise his interest.

By this time, they surely did and to the popular acclaim of the local media and, more importantly, the fans, a chirpy Cockney moved into industrial South Yorkshire. As Dave discovered and they quickly recognised, the two types aren't so very different. In fact, they are similar in that both call the proverbial spade a spade. Evidence of this was the firm friendship Bassett formed with his boardroom ally Derek Dooley, the legendary Sheffield football hero who was a record goalscorer with Wednesday before tragically losing a leg. Derek had somehow seamlessly been welcomed across the city after the Owls had brutally sacked him as manager on Christmas Eve, 1973. He was a lovely bloke who was also a constant help to me . . . even if he did once vote for me to be banned, which is a story I'll save for later!

Bassett was a joy to work with from day one. You could always get hold of him even if you had to ring a few times. Quite simply, he was never off the phone. In everything he did, he was just a ball of energy. Changes came in a flood of transfer traffic that only he could keep up with. Initially, the overhaul didn't work and United dropped into the third tier. Typical of the man, Dave (known as 'Harry' but I always felt the nickname should be reserved for his closest friends) was ready to take the blame and offer his resignation.

In hindsight, this was a crisis point for his career considering he was on rebound from the ill-fated venture at Watford where he lasted only half a season. Thankfully and wisely, United chairman Reg Brealey took Dooley's advice and backed Bassett. The rest, as they say, is history. Incidentally, it was the first time I'd ever heard a manager call his chairman 'son'—and the last! 'Are you alright, son?' said Dave as Reg came past during one of his press conferences. But then Dave called every male member of the species 'son', young and old, and Reg, who was always able to laugh at his own expense, took it in the spirit intended.

Some of Bassett's language—actually a good portion of it—was absolutely unprintable. But not unbroadcastable as viewers of a BBC fly-on-the-wall documentary were to discover. Dave could lacerate with truth and commonsense delivered in the most colourful fashion. But his players took it because he was up front and because, underneath, he had a heart of gold. So it's not hard to understand why this manager was such an inspirational figure in the dressing room as a new team, including a brilliant strike pair in Brian Deane and Tony Agana, ripped up two divisions in the quickest possible time.

Journalists were inspired by him, too. We couldn't get enough of him . . . except that often you were left with too much material. But Dave was no hothead. Like Ron Atkinson, he was calculating in the way he behaved. As his assistant Geoff Taylor would tell me, 'Harry will put on different heads for different occasions'. For instance, he was a speaker on motivational techniques and an informative pundit on television. His management was clever, even though it often seemed off-the-cuff and purely instinctive. There was a bit of that, though. He would often name the team on Friday and then change it overnight.

There was the odd cross word but it was only ever heat-of-the-moment. One night I covered a game at Derby in which United had come from behind to claim a deserved point with an equaliser from Deane. Dave used to read the *Daily Express*, who I worked for at the time. In fact, to my great gratitude, he had put a word in for me with the sports editor, David Emery. When I called him the morning after the Derby game, he had the hump—as he called it.

'What fucking game were you at last night, son?' he said. 'You've made it sound like Derby should have won—but we were the better side.' Dave had a point (in more ways than one). But what he didn't know—and this is where exchanges like this can prove useful—is that most of my report had needed to be filed by half-time. And Derby had enjoyed the better of the first half. The deadlines for night games were—and still are despite so-called advances in technology—quite an eye-opener for the uninitiated. They vary according to geography and whatever region has to be served first, so Dave had seen an early edition which didn't do justice to the way his side stormed the second half. In fact, Deane's goal was tagged on almost as an incidental detail. Bassett went up even further in my estimation for accepting this. I understood his point while he appreciated the frustrating limitations of my job.

Another time his help to me blew up in both our faces. This was before Sheffield United played a return game with Paul Gascoigne's Tottenham Hotspur at Bramall Lane. After the White Hart Lane encounter, Bassett had caused a rumpus by branding Gazza a 'buffoon'. Naturally, the media were on the case for their next meeting and the *Express* pushed me for an angle. Dave played ball to an extent but was unusually guarded. He balanced his earlier judgment by praising Gazza's undisputed skill as a player.

This wasn't enough for certain people at the *Express*. They twisted my story and had Bassett turning full circle by 'killing Gazza with kindness' and hailing him as 'a genius'—a word he had never said—in a back page-lead on the morning of the game. I was mortified to see it and took pre-emptive action by ringing Dave before he had a chance to pick up the phone to me. 'I was just about to call you, son,' he said ominously. But he heard me out and, after I'd complained to the *Express*, the sports editor wrote a letter clarifying that the version used did not reflect my original story.

Although this wasn't absolutely necessary in that I could tell Dave trusted me, I still felt both of us had been badly let down and that those responsible should get a rocket. It's par for the course that headlines can get you into trouble—however irritating that can be when they twist the meaning of your story. And, by the way, journalists don't write the headlines that appear on their stories, contrary to popular belief. But actually making up quotes for convenience is, I'm happy to say, largely a thing of the past in my experience. Quite right, too.

Dave would help in all sorts of ways. For someone who was reckoned to be a bit of a bull in a china shop, his ability to massage delicate situations was extraordinary. Here's one example. I wanted to set up an interview with Nathan Blake, a Welsh striker signed during the later stages of Bassett's reign. Dave, who was never averse to his players talking, wasn't around that particular day but a member of the administration staff obliged with Blake's number on an unofficial basis.

When I rang Nathan at his home he seemed startled to be contacted.

'Where did you get the number?' he asked.

I went into a routine that had worked well in the past. 'I really can't remember,' I said. 'I've had the number for quite a while and can't recall how I got it.'

At this, Blake rapped: 'You can't have had it for a while. I've just moved into a new house and I've only had this number for a couple of days.' Blake filled the ensuing awkward silence by demanding to know where I had got the number. I refused to tell him and a stand-off resulted.

'I'll do the interview but only if you tell me where you got the number,' he said. 'It's private and you shouldn't have it.' I tried to talk him round but he was adamant, even though he gave me a time to meet him at the ground if I had second thoughts. I heard that Blake made an issue of the incident at the club. On the appointed day I bumped into Bassett outside the ground and told him of the problem without naming the person who had assisted with the number. He said he could only help if I told him. I reluctantly did so but only on the proviso that the person concerned would not get into trouble. Dave agreed and the interview took place as if nothing had happened. What I was more concerned about was the other part of the arrangement, but I needn't have worried. All Dave did was ask a certain member of the admin team to send round a memo to all staff making it clear that in no circumstances were players' numbers to be released. Nothing more was said and yet the point had been made. Brilliant.

I felt such loyalty towards Bassett that I took up cudgels against chairman Brealey, with whom I'd always got on fairly amicably, over a shortage of cash for new players. It's fair to say I kept hitting Brealey over the head with a series of critical articles in both the *Daily Express* and the *Sheffield Telegraph*, where I'd just started to contribute local columns. Some of what I said was right, but the way I did it was wrong. If you make your point once, people will accept it as fair comment. If you keep repeating it over and over again, they will have you down as a troublemaker.

I failed to heed a friendly warning from Dooley who was very much on Bassett's side and probably in agreement with much of what I was writing. 'Don't keep going over it again and again,' Derek told me with the telling rider: 'If you live by the sword you'll die by it.' This was fair warning from a friend rather than a foe but I failed to take notice. The final straw was a *Sheffield Telegraph* piece in which I opened with a reference to the 'clownish face' of the club and which had the damning headline 'Send in the Clowns'. Unintentionally, this could only be interpreted as a slight on everyone in the boardroom, Dooley included. I don't blame him for raising his hand—as he openly admitted to me that he did—when Brealey took a vote on whether I should be banned.

Unbeknown to me, the vote took place on a Friday morning in advance of Dave Bassett's regular pre-match press conference. It was a fine day and I was among a group of journalists waiting outside in the car park ready to move into Dave's office. Finally, he strolled across from another part of the building, made a beeline for me and said: 'I believe you're banned, son.' I thought he was joking at first but Dave confirmed the news and followed up: 'So I think we'll do this press conference here in the car park.' It was his way of allowing me to attend and a magnificent gesture of support for which I was extremely grateful. Again, this was typical of him and the sort of loyalty that inspired his players. Sheffield's *Green 'Un* sports paper followed up with the headline: 'Alan out but the Banned played on . . . '

With Bassett's help, and the quiet support of Dooley, who had made his stand as a token gesture, the row quickly blew over. Derek and secretary Dave Capper would make a joke of it. Whenever I appeared at the ground, they would wave their arms frantically and pretend to order me out. But I still had not fully learned my lesson. After one more attack on Brealey, I was informed on a Friday afternoon that I was banned once more. This time, Dooley felt it was unnecessarily harsh and offered to help.

Nothing happened at first so I decided to phone Reg at home that evening. The point was that the following day I was booked to work at Bramall Lane for Radio 5 Live, *BBC Look North*, the *Sunday Express* and the *Daily Express*. In fact, it would be easier to list who I *wasn't* working for. These were great days, quite lucrative, although I sometimes wonder how I managed to do it all without having a heart attack. Perhaps just as well I'm usually limited to just one or two matchday assignments these days.

Anyway, Reg had his answerphone on so I left a message to the effect that if I was banned I would have to ring all these media organisations (I listed them) to explain why I would not be able to attend the game. The inference was that all of them would carry the story. It worked a treat. Within seconds, Reg rang back to say he wasn't happy but that I could come to the match. And that marked a truce in our relationship.

The truth is that I always liked Reg and still do. Even more so in that whenever I've bumped into him in recent times he's always prepared to laugh at all those rows. But I've also made a point of saying sorry to him, which is something I'm now happy to repeat because, although the club did become chaotic under him at one stage and he certainly blundered by selling Deane to Leeds, he did contribute a good deal of time and money and always had United's best interests at heart.

Bassett was never short of a word or two hundred but there was one time he was rendered speechless—at least to the media, which was almost unheard of. Remarkably, too, it was after a victory. The Blades had beaten Nottingham Forest 3–2 in December 1990. This was not any old win. It was United's first season back in the top flight—and their first three points after months of trying.

The normally ebullient Bassett had confessed in an interview with me a few days previously that he was 'living a nightmare' with his team marooned at the bottom and seemingly sunk. So when the final whistle blew after a nerve-shredding finale to the Forest game, we waited as usual for Bassett at the end of the dressing room corridor. He often took his time but it was always worth the wait. On this occasion we waited . . . and waited. Finally, the message came through that he would be sending out players instead.

The reason, it later emerged, was that Dave had opened a bottle of scotch and he was not going to shift until it was emptied! I don't think his family saw him that night, either. Incidentally, that game—which triggered one of the greatest relegation escapes of all time—was the one occasion when I came anywhere within close proximity of the great Brian Clough. He had become a reclusive figure with the media at that stage, rarely, if ever, giving interviews. But he had to pass us on the way out of Bramall Lane. We simply gawped as he strode by, knowing it was pointless to attempt a conversation. But as he reached us he suddenly stopped in his tracks. 'Merry Christmas, gentlemen,' he beamed. At that point a couple of mouths opened to try to engage the great man. He parried with 'and I say, "Merry Christmas, gentlemen"' and strode off into the night. Believe it or not, I wrote it all down . . . as you can tell.

Extra, extra, read all about it! No, not that story. This is the tale of my only other Clough connection—which was very much by proxy. A football journalist finds himself at many loose ends during the close-season. So it was that during the summer of 2008, I signed up as an extra for a day's shooting on *The Damned United*, the film about Ol' Big 'Ead's 44 days as successor to Don Revie at Leeds. This was underpaid and overworked—about £40 for 12 hours of shouting yourself hoarse as a fan on the terraces. But it was worth it for the proper work I netted as a result, including a colour piece for retro magazine *Backpass*. And even more worth it for just 'being there'.

During that day in pouring rain—and half the night—I was among 150 crowd scene volunteers who were rotated around my beloved Saltergate, chosen because of its resemblance to Derby's old home at the Baseball Ground. We were variously cast as fans of Leeds, Derby or other clubs like Arsenal and with clever editing, our small rent-a-crowd made it look in the film like the place was full. All the while Michael Sheen (Clough) and Timothy Spall (Peter Taylor) played the lead roles in front of us, along with a collection of footballing actors who were much better suited as lookalikes than play-a-likes. Scenes would repeatedly have to be re-shot as they fluffed their 'lines' on game sequences.

Back to Bassett. The only other time I recall him being lost for words was following United's shock relegation of 1994. This was because he was absolutely devastated, totally distraught. Before that final day, it seemed so improbable that the Blades would drop that Dave was clearly preparing for a party. He was in relaxed mood in his office on the eve of the game. In fact, he gave each of us a bottle of champagne (proper stuff) so that we could celebrate with him. But this wasn't really about a manager dropping his guard or taking things for granted. It was actually a thank you for working closely with him and, as such, a magnificent gesture that was truly appreciated. So everyone was genuinely gutted for Dave about what followed.

I was covering a game for BBC radio at Hillsborough and felt sick to my stomach as the events unfolded. The fact that United lost should have been irrelevant. Their demise had more to do with a lethal cocktail of other results which all went against them in the most unlikely fashion. Most improbable of all was Everton—who were desperately struggling at the time—coming from behind to beat Bassett's old team, Wimbledon, with two late goals at Goodison Park that later raised murmurs of suspicion about Dons keeper Hans Segers amid match-fixing allegations against Liverpool's Bruce Grobbelaar, which were subsequently unproven in a court case that cleared him.

Dave was left with a nasty taste in his mouth but kept his tongue still. Although the conspiracy theories have been laid to rest, relegation was hard to swallow.

This effectively marked the end of the golden era at Bramall Lane, confirmed by Deane's £2.7m sale to Leeds (when Sheffield Wednesday were offering £3.1m) and eventually Bassett's departure by mutual consent. We kept in touch because, like so many sporting celebrities who moved to Sheffield (including Chris Waddle, Emlyn Hughes and Carlton Palmer), he found this so-called grimy northern city a real eye-opener. It borders magnificent countryside in the leafy western fringes and has become something of a venus flytrap for football personalities.

By chance, Dave moved to a house within 200 yards of mine, which was also just around the corner from Waddle. A discreet distance was observed but I'd often bump into each of them for random chats in the village and—in a stretch of my own rule and I suspect his, too—I enjoyed a few lunchtime pints with Dave on a couple of occasions when he was between jobs. Others who lived nearby over the years were former United stars Brian Gayle and Simon Tracey and ex-Wednesday skipper Trond Soltvedt. Of course, there had to be advantages and there were times when I couldn't help but trip over stories just by walking out of my front door!

10

THE ODD COUPLE: FRANCIS AND BASSETT

As boss of the Blades, Dave Bassett enjoyed a good deal of knockabout banter with rival manager Ron Atkinson while they were in opposition across the city's great divide. But this relationship had nothing like the warmth that developed between Dave and Trevor Francis, who was promoted from the dressing room as Ron's replacement at Hillsborough in 1991. They couldn't have been more different. Bassett had literally scrapped his way up from the basement, having to play the sort of football that a disdainful Francis probably frowned on at the time. Trevor, England's first £1m player, was urbane, elegant, slightly cool and supposedly aloof. He was the quiet family man, a private figure who didn't have to shout from the rooftops for the recognition that was naturally accorded to his celebrated career. He was a European Cup winner for Brian Clough's Nottingham Forest, scoring the winning goal in the first of their triumphs, and, as an England international with 52 caps, Francis was among the top players of his generation. Consider the contrast with Bassett whose playing career was purely non-league. Before they actually got to meet, I suspect they probably had an equally dispassionate view of each other.

The media seized on their chalk-and-cheese background ahead of the all-Sheffield FA Cup semi-final in 1993. Even after a couple of years as managerial rivals, the distance between them seemed just as great. The *Express* lobbed a grenade in my direction by commissioning me to ask each of them about each other. I started with the easier one and went to Dave. He was generous, without being lavish, in his praise for the job Trevor was doing at Wednesday.

Great. This'll work, I thought, if I can get Trevor to do the same. He seemed nonplussed by the question at first and at a loss to follow suit. For political reasons, there was no way I wanted one to praise the other and the other one to throw it back in his face. It might have been a better story for today but it didn't bode well for tomorrow. So I'm not ashamed to say that I, shall we say, massaged the interview with Trevor just a little and also the quotes that followed. The *Express* headline ran along the lines of a Francis-Bassett love-in, with the rider: 'You're great, they tell each other.' But this was better for all concerned than the opposite. Peace in our time!

Whether fanciful or not, I like to think that article helped bring these two opposites together. In truth, I believe Trevor was only cautious because he really didn't know Dave—whereas Bassett was always more adept at dishing out quotes that fitted. Lo and behold, within a few months they were best buddies and visiting each other for dinner parties!

Journalistically, they required different handling, which is part of the skill and also the attraction of the job. Knowing Trevor a little as a player helped, of course. There was also knowledge of his previous managerial misadventure at Queens Park Rangers where he fell out with players who were said to have considered him too high-handed and dictatorial. At Hillsborough Trevor was actually promoted from the dressing room and, whether this was a factor or not, he appeared to make a point of modifying his style. And it worked a treat.

By the end, his approach may have seemed a little too lenient as he was undermined by player power and a dressing room clique that David Pleat was left with the job of breaking up. But in between, Francis proved himself to be a formidable operator. It was no easy task filling Big Ron's shoes. Trevor brought subtlety and intelligence to the role, carefully maintaining the status quo and adding to it so that Wednesday qualified for Europe and reached both domestic cup finals in the 1992–93 season.

He also became adept at PR, which had not been regarded as one of his strengths at Loftus Road. Trevor had obviously noted Atkinson's ease with the media and slipped seamlessly into a positive relationship. This was after one early blip. Francis had been linked with a move to sign the Glasgow Rangers and England goalkeeper, Chris Woods. I rang Trevor to check out the story and he put me off the scent. The following day, I joined the rest of the media corps at Hillsborough—for Woods' unveiling as a Wednesday player.

On arrival, I challenged Francis in the car park and made clear my thoughts. In fairness, Trevor had only acted in the way that many managers have done before and since by not wanting to show his hand for fear of losing a transfer coup. But I pointed out that I would have much preferred an off-the-record steer or even a 'no comment', which can be both helpful and appreciated. He listened to the complaint without taking umbrage and there was to be no repeat. 'Tricky Trevor,' as he had become known by Wednesday fans in deference to his skills as a player, played it by the book. Not that there is one, of course. It's a case of making it up as you go along.

There can never be any hard and fast rules for managers in their media relations. It is something they have to learn over the years and the same applies in reverse to reporters. An approach that might work in one situation might backfire in another. So the teething trouble with Trevor was quite normal, I feel. The mistake would have been to say nothing and let it linger. Clearing the air in a reasonable way like this helps both sides get a clearer understanding.

It also helped me with Trevor, I think, that I had a regular page in the *Sheffield Telegraph* where I could be more analytical and sympathetic to the sort of problems he was to face—by contrast with the more black-and-white approach demanded by the nationals. Balancing the two was a tricky part of my regular work pattern, but it was a definite advantage to be able to go into more depth on the local front.

Throughout his four years at Wednesday Trevor was easy-going and engaging company. He always tried to help even if he didn't have Ron's gift for choosing his own angle, or his predecessor's sense of drama. Except for one occasion I will never forget. It was during a sleepy summer in 1992 that I rang Trevor on some pretext I can't recall. Basically, I was just ferreting for a story—as always!

Trevor answered a couple of routine queries and then dropped a bombshell into the conversation. 'I'm trying to sign Chris Waddle,' he said flatly. And he proceeded to tell me he had made an opening approach to Marseilles, Waddle's club in France. Gathering my composure after such a dramatic revelation, I blinked the pound signs out of my eyes and asked whether he was telling me this off the record. 'Oh, no,' he said, 'you can quote me if you want.' And he went on to outline all the reasons why he wanted Waddle at Hillsborough and why he thought he could pull it off.

To this day, I remain amazed at Trevor's openness. This was the first anyone had heard of a Wednesday bid for one of England's top players. There had only been a rumoured link between Waddle and his former club Newcastle—but potential competition like that, considering Chris's North East background, made it even stranger that Francis was declaring his hand in such a way. But, as the saying goes, never look a gift horse in the mouth. Needless to say, I made a killing on that story which remains the best unprompted transfer tale anyone has ever dropped into my lap. Whatever Trevor's rationale, I thanked him profusely, of course. He could have chosen to tell someone else. And he was right to be confident because Waddle duly signed for Wednesday following protracted negotiations later that summer.

Chairing a sports forum in 1975 with (from left to right) Barrie Leadbeater (Yorkshire batsman), Mick Prendergast (Sheffield Wednesday striker), Bob Brenton (Sports Editor, Radio Sheffield), Dennis Amiss (England Test batsman), Derek Dooley (Mr Sheffield Football)

Interviewing Gordon Banks, 1966 hero in '76

On the receiving end after another smash-hit victory from Herol 'Bomber' Graham

Slaving over hot turntables at Radio Hallam circa 1983

'They Like you!'

Question of Sport Roadshow in Chesterfield, October 1981. From left, me, Mike Firth (local journalist), Ron Pickering and Emlyn Hughes. The MC is BBC rugby commentator Ian Robertsson

Eyes down, look in for ringside boxing commentary. Flanked from left to right by Ken Knighton, Stuart Linnell and my late friend Derrick Connolly, the chief engineer who gave me my biggest ever rollocking!

Looking to the heavens with pilot Robin Batchelor before
a hot air balloon flight over Sheffield

'New rule needed: bbw—balloon before wicket!'

Paradise Perch—blissful cricket reporting from the pavilion balcony at Queen's Park, Chesterfield. Above is the clock that a flustered Dickie Bird, wielding a broom handle remonstrated with the author to put right

'Howzat?' 'Out!'

As MC for a snooker charity event featuring Patsy Fagan (second from right) and the legendary Fred Davies (second from left)

'All I said was maybe you should just stick to hunting, fishing and football'

Interviewing 1979 world snooker champion Terry Griffiths. Looking on is one of the great press box characters Alan Thompson of the *Daily Express*. The late 'Thommo' struck fear in players and managers for his forthright views but was a real gentleman underneath

'We interrupt this 147 to bring you a commercial break . . .'

'Calls himself a reporter! Glad they threw away the key!'

The author on home ground

© Trevor Smith Photography

Hey, there were plenty of times when other journalists scooped me on stories, so forgive my self-indulgence. Just like a match editor on television, you only select the highlights! Besides, I've always thought reporters should be judged more on the stories they *get* rather than those they *miss*. It was more the other way round at one time on the Yorkshire patch. As a freelance, I've tried to reverse that psychology. But that was a luxury the staff guys couldn't afford. As I discovered during a year on contract with the *Express* and later, in a retainer attachment with the *Daily Mail*, the main pressure was to ensure you didn't miss something the others had. I found this stifling and eventually broke free of that system.

TF is a man of hidden depths. Some people have viewed him as cold fish, but those who've had the pleasure of getting to know him will tell you he is a warm, humorous character with a fun-loving nature. I found him to be quite laid back most of the time but, again, this masked the steely resolve that made him a perfectionist as a player. And if he said he was going to do something, he would do it. Witness the Waddle coup. Another example came during a chat in his office early in his reign while he was still player-manager. It was for a feature-type piece in the *Sunday Express*, agreed on the basis that he approved the content.

His thoughts were reasoned as usual, but going nowhere in particular when, more in hope than expectation, I asked when he might hang up his boots . . . and bang, there was the line! He had, he said, almost certainly made his last appearance as a player. I doubt the announcement was pre-planned but I was proud and privileged to get this scoop. Although the news had been widely hinted, this was the first time Trevor had gone public with his thoughts. It always makes a bit of a splash when such a big name calls it quits. While there had been plenty of speculation, this was Trevor choosing his moment. Well, actually, that may not be right. I feel it was an instinctive act and, rather like some of his many goals, executed on the spur of the moment.

Unlikely though this may seem, these were days when you

could just drop in off the street to interview star players at football grounds after they'd finished training. Hence some great relationships were struck with Wednesday players like David Hirst, Nigel Worthington, Mel Sterland, Nigel Pearson, John Sheridan, Lawrie Madden, Mark Smith and Chris Turner. In fact, most of the lads of that era were a pleasure to deal with and I'm only sorry I can't name them all. Likewise at Bramall Lane where star strikers Brian Deane and Tony Agana led the media agenda on and off the field. I was particularly grateful for relationships formed with goalkeeping rivals Alan Kelly and Simon Tracey, while skipper Brian Gayle was also a great ambassador for the Blades.

Wednesday's Glynn Snodin, in particular, was a real treasure, always willing to talk whatever the result. Thankfully every club seems to have one like him. Wilkinson twigged this when I pulled him once to talk down the line to a chap in the studio at Clubcall, which at the time was an in-house service for Wednesday fans. For some reason, the interviewer had got his wires crossed and thought I'd told him it was going to be Glynn at the other end—as was often the case. Thus Howard was introduced as the team's likeable left-back—and impishly decided to play the part. 'Gaffer's had a right pop at us,' he opened in true Snodin style. And it was some while later, with me looking on in stitches, before he suddenly paused and said matter-of-factly: 'It's Howard.'

Of all the stars at the Sheffield clubs, the relationship I probably guarded most jealously was with Hirst. He was a youngster when he came from Barnsley and I helped nurse him through a few early interviews where he seemed too shy to say anything much for himself and had to be prompted. A few years later, when he emerged as a terrific striker on course for England honours, he quietly came up and asked me: 'Can you look after me?' I hope I did. It was perhaps largely due to this that an emotional David came and put his arms round me at a London hotel reception after he'd scored in the 1993 FA Cup final with Arsenal. I was truly touched by the gesture. Of course, David is better known as a bit of a jack-the-lad, a fun-loving side he hid from us in his early years even though we knew he always liked a pint. And what's wrong with that?

'Hirsty' showed his true colours after an ill-advised story involving (rather than written by) me about a possible UFO sighting over the outskirts of Sheffield. My son joined me in gazing at the strange spectacle from a back bedroom window. As many other witnesses verified, there were indeed bright lights in the sky—but I was embarrassed, to say the least, when experts reckoned these were nothing more than the white feather patches under the wings of pigeons! This seemed even more implausible than aliens at the time, but I guess it was all a strange trick of the light. Or I'd gone cuckoo!

My mobile rang a few days later and an unfamiliar voice announced: 'Mr Biggs, I'm Professor Smythe from Jodrell Bank and I'd like, if I may, to talk to you about your UFO sighting.' Stupidly, I thought this was genuine and told the 'professor' I'd be happy to discuss it. 'It's Hirsty!' he said.

A hasty retreat back to Trevor Francis whose reign eventually began to fragment amid some public attacks on his methods by high-profile players who inferred his man-management was poor. I remember interviewing Chris Woods after he had been dropped and the goalkeeper joined the list of dissenting voices. I felt uneasy about doing that story, even though you could not ignore the general rumblings. But Trevor was never resentful, respecting that you had a job to do. And I felt sorry for him, especially after a sickening back page splash in a Sunday tabloid based on an interview with an unnamed player. The source said senior players wanted Chris Waddle to take charge. In short, a mutiny! And so began the episode of the hunt for the infamous 'Hillsborough mole'. Needless to say, he went to ground. It was all pretty despicable, not to say unnecessary because results continued to keep Wednesday in a respectable position in the Premiership and Francis's overall record was extremely impressive.

Trevor handled the dressing room sniping calmly, almost as if it didn't bother him, which I suspect inflamed some players even more. But I felt then, as I still do today, that he was owed greater loyalty by those stars—considering they enjoyed some of the best years of their career under Francis. And Dave Richards' board should have had the strength to back their manager rather than taking the easy way out. They would, I am convinced, have been far better off in the long run. It's even more absurd now than it was at the time to think that Francis was sacked for finishing 13th in the Premier League. What would the Owls give for such a lofty perch today—or in most of the intervening years, for that matter?

The method of Trevor's removal was even more unsavoury. Richards and his directors decided on a change weeks ahead of the end of the 1994–95 season. This was their prerogative. What was shameful was that they made it an open secret by blatantly encouraging speculation on a replacement and Trevor had to endure it all as a dead man walking. Here he showed his dignity and class.

Naturally, I joined in the name game. There was no option, really. I felt strongly that the best man for the job was Dave Bassett who by this time was on the way out at Bramall Lane. The downside was that he would be a controversial appointment—but this gave it even higher value as a speculative story. Just a hint that Wednesday would actually consider Bassett was all we needed. Several of us went down that line, even though Dave tried his best to stop the story. Normally, he was not averse to the sort of outside speculation that might strengthen his hand—but his friendship with Trevor made this scenario different. We went ahead and I remember meeting with an icy reaction from Mick Mills, the former England skipper who was on Francis's staff at Hillsborough, when the Bassett link was floated. He thought it was disrespectful to the man in situ and I had to agree in many ways. But I pointed out that it was only fair game to us because of the way Wednesday's board had behaved.

Typically, Trevor understood and never raised a murmur. He somehow managed to stay above it all. Nevertheless there were pangs of conscience when he invited the local media corps to a sort of unofficial leaving party in one of the Hillsborough offices after the final game of the 1994–95 season. He was still in charge but the whispering campaign had left him in no doubt his reign was effectively over. Trevor's lovely wife Helen was there among family and friends. That was a measure of how this private man had accepted a handful of journalists as people he clearly liked and trusted. And it goes without saying that I am truly honoured he agreed to write the foreword for this book. My abiding memory of that farewell occasion was seeing Richards shuffle past the open door and momentarily cast a sheepish glance inside.

Still there was no immediate confirmation of Francis's fate and it only came—surprise, surprise—on FA Cup Final day. You would have thought that the people who make these decisions—as they are fully entitled to do, by the way—would show some moral courage and not try to hide behind the timing. Incredibly, Atkinson's demise of three years later was to be handled in the same shameful manner . . . announced while the nation's eyes and ears were on Wembley. Richards (later Sir Dave) went on to become chairman of the Premier League and, with key Football Association roles to boot, easily the most powerful figure in the English game. And this in spite of Wednesday's eventual demise, which started under his leadership, and the collapse of his engineering business. Enough said perhaps.

By way of balance, it has to be acknowledged that Richards helped to break the mould at Hillsborough. He launched an ambitious approach after taking over from Bert McGee, a formidable but likeable character who always had the club's interests at heart. As an old school figure, McGee stood aside when Wednesday were breaking new ground under Atkinson.

Richards happily danced to Big Ron's tune and kept Wednesday competitive in the transfer market under Francis, if not among the biggest spenders. At the outset, I found the new chairman to be open and accessible. Later, he would be 'unavailable' and efforts to talk to him could take weeks on end. But you had to respect the progress made under his chairmanship and I still do up to a point. Except that the club must have overstretched its resources because Wednesday's long decline is plainly rooted in that period of profligacy. Richards made his escape in 1999 with his club on the slide from the top flight. To an extent, I sympathised when, ahead of an invitation to take the Premier League chair, he couldn't do right for doing wrong. Wednesday were debt-ridden and about to go into freefall, and fans were calling for Richards to quit. Then they accused him of deserting a sinking shift when he took the Premiership position. Hang on, you can't have it both ways.

But Richards had a tendency to try to be all things to all men, which possibly explains a meteoric rise that otherwise defies all logic and the reason why the Premier League's warring factions saw him as the ideal peacemaker. For instance, he would often tell me face to face 'if you ever need me just give me a call'. This, as I've described, was easier said than done. When Wednesday's debt level became gravely apparent but largely unspecified, I sought out Richards for clarification.

There was no response to requests through the club. So I took the bold step of publishing a list of questions in the *Sheffield Telegraph* that I felt Richards should answer. The headline told Richards that it was 'time to answer the questions, Mr Chairman'. In response, Alan Sykes, the club secretary, suggested I had now blown any chance of speaking to the chairman. What neither of them knew was that if that proved to be the case then we planned to run a blank space the following week under the headline: 'Richards' response to the *Telegraph*'. Then came a surprise development.

A new press officer at the club, Sue Hesk, quickly made her mark by persuading Richards to face up. Whether she suspected how we would play it if he didn't, I don't know. So I was summoned to a meeting at the ground, thinking it might be a bit like the Gunfight at the OK Corral. The reality could not have been more different. Both of us were armed—but only with a copy of the previous week's paper where the questions were listed.

Friendliness personified, Dave put on his glasses and, peering over them, said: 'No problem. I can answer these questions. Anytime you want to speak to me you only have to call, you know.' I didn't reply, as perhaps I should, but the reason why we had to meet in these circumstances was that you couldn't simply pick up the phone. There followed a very honest disclosure of Wednesday's financial position, amid an undertaking from me that we would treat the information with respect and would endeavour to take a positive approach. This we did and the proceeds of that session, which revealed a club debt of around £17m, ran for a couple of weeks.

I should also add that Richards, who clearly doesn't relish confrontation, has always been cordial on the rare occasions we have bumped into each other over the years. You have to respect the fact that he can take criticism on the chin, not to mention that there must be something to merit his reflected glory in presiding over the Premier League's development into the richest and most watched league in the world. And he has certainly managed to unite some powerful interests. Yet it is hard to find anyone in football who has a good word to say about Dave Richards, which is pretty amazing in itself. Maybe I know the wrong people! But I do wonder how he has managed to navigate himself into such an exalted position. Many a newspaper columnist has rated it among the mysteries of our time and I can't say I disagree with them.

At least, however, I'm in a position to acknowledge his early impact as Sheffield Wednesday chairman. Incredible as it now seems, the club transformed itself from a cautious, staid outfit into one that attracted big name internationals like Waddle and Des Walker. The latter was noted for rarely, if ever, doing interviews. For all that he was a cheery character who'd always smile and say hello, the only proper chat I ever had with him was on the day of his unveiling as a £2.75m signing from Sampdoria in 1993. He was hardly in a position to keep his mouth shut at his own press conference and I found him to be quite a self-effacing character.

Waddle, too, is known to have suffered from shyness but once you get him talking he is hard to stop—as 5 Live listeners would testify. From a somewhat rambling start, Chris has become a terrific pundit, always passionate and informative. Dealing with him at Hillsborough was mostly a pleasure. I got to know him slightly by regularly ringing his hotel room in Sheffield before he bought a house in my neighbourhood. I should add there are few other similarities between our abodes!

Anyway, Chris would happily serve up some decent quotes and something of a relationship developed. After one victory in a cup game with Derby County, he even stopped by for a chat without being asked. I'd been hanging around at the end of the dressing room corridor as various players came through. What Chris couldn't have known was that I was specifically waiting for Paul Warhurst, the scorer of the winning goal that night. Warhurst was actually a centre back but was in such an extraordinary scoring streak as Francis's inspired choice as emergency stand-in for the injured David Hirst that he was on his way to an incredible call up by England—as a striker! What I wanted to ask on this particular night was whether Warhurst now actually regarded himself as a forward, or whether he would prefer to return eventually to his normal position.

Let me further explain that Paul would often slip away unnoticed after games. He never seemed to relish the spotlight. So it was with one eye on the exit door behind Waddle that I stood and spoke to Chris. This was something of a dilemma because I was being honoured by one of the greats of the game, for which I was truly appreciative. Then Warhurst darted through behind Chris with his head down, making a beeline for the car park outside. Instinctively, I headed after him while blurting an apology to Chris, who, judging by subsequent events, either didn't hear or it or thought it was insufficient to cover my sudden loss of interest.

I passed Chris walking through the stand past the players' bar later that night and tried to say sorry again but he clearly thought I was being rude. Looking back, I don't blame him if he felt put out. In his shoes, I think I'd have felt affronted. At face value, here was a celebrated England international being stood up by a journalist who should have been glad of his company. Which I was. It was all a clumsy misunderstanding which resulted from the pressures of the job.

Chris was less available after that, not only to me but to others as well. Happily, it was only a passing phase and I think he realises that no personal slight was intended. We've done interviews since then and, living so close by, we'll occasionally have a chat on a street corner. That's as far as I've tried to take it, though. Not because I don't enjoy his company, which I do, but because it's not always the ideal world it would seem to live so close to subjects of your professional attention. And I don't flatter myself, either, that someone like Waddle would want my company in a social sense. As I've said, Dave Bassett, too, lived in the same suburb at one stage and we'd often bump into each other. But it was only after he left Sheffield United that we met for a pint on a couple of occasions.

People might think I'm a pretty poor journalist not looking to take undue advantage of dream-like circumstances like these. But I think you gain more from keeping your distance and not trying to close in on public figures; certainly, I found this approach produced the best results. Besides, I've always believed in observing other people's privacy in the same way that I like my own to be respected. The ends don't justify the means in my book. There's a right way and a wrong way of doing things.

11

BET YOU CAN'T GUESS WHO
I MET TODAY . . .

Without being blasé, rubbing shoulders with celebrities was almost a daily occurrence back at Radio Hallam in the late Seventies and early Eighties. You'd find yourself sharing a lift with Rod Stewart on his way up to do an interview or pass Cliff Richard in the studio corridor. What was more daunting was actually forming their acquaintance while you were on air reading the news or the sports desk.

The studio was cramped which meant you were even closer to these stars. On one occasion, I squeezed in alongside Sandie Shaw, the Sixties pop star and former Eurovision winner, to present a sports update. Sandie was clearly a bubbly person but she kept dutifully quiet . . . until the result of a particular horse race from Kempton or wherever. The winner was Lady Wood. So it went like this . . . 'Kempton Park, the 3.15, first number six Lady Wood . . . '

At which point Sandie burst out: 'Oh no, she wouldn't!' Try keeping a straight face and a steady voice after that. These days that would be considered good broadcasting—and I've no doubt it was entertaining at the time, not least to me. But this was before the style of seamless, mix and match banter where presenters strategically interrupt sports desks to maintain a casual, conversational flow. Back then, the two things were largely separate, barring exchanges with the presenter before and after.

Sometimes, I would grab visiting celebrities to talk about sport. Tommy Steele and Frankie Vaughan somehow fell into this category . . . I can't remember why! Other visitors like Henry Cooper, Barry Sheene and Don Revie, who joined me for an hour live in the studio, were more up my street—while great Olympians were no stranger to our studios either. This was courtesy of local decathlete Mike Corden, a great character who I'd recruited to do a keep-fit slot. Mike was a real man about town—and still is from what I discovered when I bumped into him aboard a cruise ship a couple of years ago—and I would have a burst of Fred Wedlock's song 'The Oldest Swinger in Town' lined up for whenever he put in an appearance. There was more slapstick than fitness information about this spot because, among other things, we sang Christmas carols live on air one December. However the listeners put up with us, I'll never know.

Anyway, Mike was well connected and, thanks to him, I had surprise visits from double Olympic gold medal winner Daley Thompson and shot-putter Geoff Capes. In each case, we went off to some watering hole for lunch after the interviews. Daley was a bubbly character who took the attention in his stride, but Geoff came over as very intense and didn't relish being recognised. Also around that time, Ken Dodd offered a tattyfilarious view of football when I interviewed him in his dressing room at Sheffield's then Fiesta nightclub.

But the showbiz interview to end them all, at least as far as I was concerned, took place at the Donington Park racetrack in 1978. No disrespect to Jackie Stewart, who forgave my ignorance about his sport when I chatted to him, but even interviewing the former world motor racing champion just paled into insignificance beside something else that happened to me that day. I met and interviewed George Harrison. It was just one of those happy accidents that make life worth living. The former Beatle wasn't even billed to be there. Why would he be, I hear you asking. Indeed, I was to ask him that very question.

It all happened quite naturally. One of the organisers of the event—the Gunnar Nilsson Memorial Trophy—told me that Harrison was there. George loved motorsport, apparently. I knew that he was quite a reclusive character who rarely, if ever, indulged the media, so it was more in hope than expectation that I asked if I could see him. A few minutes later, a familiar figure with a fleece-lined brown jacket just materialised in front of me. No entourage, no fans around, just the two of us.

This was a pinch yourself moment for someone who had grown up as a Beatles fan. I was seven when they had their first hit and had pictures of the Fab Four all over my bedroom wall. George was a gent. He gave me four or five minutes during which his passion for motor racing came through. He told me he'd just had the chance to test drive Stirling Moss's old Lotus and George said his latest album included a number called 'Faster' as a tribute to the greats of the track. Playing this was a perfect fit when the recorded interview was relayed on Stuart Linnell's *Sportacular* programme later that Saturday afternoon—and repeated to a peaktime Sunday morning audience the next day.

Thrilled as I was in a personal sense, I was still completely unaware of the scale of this scoop. Stuart did cartwheels over it and I realised that no-one else at Hallam, including the household name deejays on the station, had interviewed a Beatle for the station. Needless to say, I kept that tape and it is available on an archive website called www.soundboard.com courtesy of former Hallam presenter Frank Carpenter, who kindly cleaned up the old cassette tape I'd kept, put it on CD for the two of us and added it to his collection of clips.

But I have to add that I was swiftly brought down to earth on that day in 1978 when I went home to tell my brother Graham— three years my junior and not so affected by Beatlemania—of my great adventure. I teased him with 'guess who I've interviewed today' and then delivered the two-word legend, George Harrison. 'Who does he play for then?' he said. Bump. Graham is usually much better for my ego and, as a sports lover himself, remains a close confidant.

Closer to home and back in the world of sport, we had an international star emerging in Sheffield around that time. Our listeners were aware of him well before he came to prominence thanks to the station's athletics expert—and also a jack of all trades—David Haywood. David worked in an accounts office but was recognised throughout the area for his knowledge of athletics and he was quick to alert us to the prodigious talent of a middle distance runner called Sebastian Newbold Coe. Along with the local papers, we monitored his progress.

But no-one could predict the overnight superstardom that would come Coe's way in 1979 when he set three world records in 41 days. After the first of these, in Oslo, I went for the first time to the home of the Coe family in Sheffield to gauge the reaction. Seb's mother Angela invited me in warmly and gushed out her pride in between taking calls . . . because the phone just never stopped ringing. At this stage, the attention was a novelty. Never having been in such a position it is difficult to understand, but I guess that the attention can quickly become a pain and that seemed to happen in this case. Whether it was because we were too pushy or they were too precious, I don't know. But I felt it was quickly forgotten that certain local media organisations had been championing Seb while he was still a nobody. Not that this is necessarily an entitlement for special treatment or an obligation to the people at the centre of it all.

Seb was a pleasant young guy—around 20—and he seemed to take it all in his stride. But his father, Peter, was fiercely protective to the point where you daren't ring the family home let alone call in. I never did repeat that first happy visit. He would snap and give you short shrift. Peter was a perfectionist coach who, famously, would also give Seb a hard time.

I'm only recalling how I found Peter rather than making a judgment because I don't know what it's like to father a celebrity or how protective that must make you feel. The Coes were clearly a close-knit, loving family and naturally Seb's welfare was all-important. But it was disappointing to be suddenly kept at a distance when we were careful not to be too intrusive. There is a tendency for media people not to respect boundaries so I suppose there are two sides to this. Seb remained gracious and charming whenever he was off the leash.

In contrast, I suppose I took the general situation much too personally and became unnecessarily petty-minded at one point. There was a spell when Radio Hallam were frozen out altogether by the Coe family. After this, we rolled over and allowed our tummies to be tickled as Seb came in for an interview on one of our daytime programmes. I pointedly blanked him. This was pathetic on my part and on reflection I'm pretty ashamed of my behaviour. You've got to be bigger than that.

When you think about it, everyone has to be handled differently. That's part of the journalist's stock-in-trade. A straightforward approach worked with another South Yorkshire athletics star, Peter Elliott, a Rotherham lad and as down-to-earth as they come. Sometimes the need is to be more subtle and that might even mean keeping your distance for a period.

Anyway, I finally made a formal and rather belated apology to the now Lord Coe, putting it down to my own relative youth at the time. It was actually the sport of netball which gave me a somewhat bizarre reason for writing to him and he sent a gracious reply. Bizarre because if anyone had told me I'd spend a couple of years as a netball commentator I'd have had them certified on the spot. I suspect probably this only happened because Televideo, the Sheffield production company, couldn't find anyone else after winning the contract to package this all-female sport for a new audience on Sky.

After a couple of years, I was a convert to the view that netball should be an Olympic sport and wrote to Seb to see if he could use his influence accordingly. The athleticism of the girls who play in the netball superleague is truly impressive. And that's not all, of course! After my mates in the pub had stopped taking the proverbial over my surprise new assignment, they became quite jealous. But I think the guy having the biggest laugh was the man upstairs: 'Let's give Biggsy the job of interviewing all these gorgeous girls . . . oh, but let's wait until he's past 50 first!'

Seriously, what I enjoyed most about my two seasons as the voice of netball—2007 to 2009—was the challenge of doing something completely different. For starters, I'd never seen a game and had to put that right by going in for special tuition at my kids' school where daughters Rosanna and Isabelle had both played. Then there was the question of how to pitch the commentary because this was the first time netball had been regularly televised in this country. It struck me that, with goals flying in at 60-odd per game, a slightly restrained approach was called for. So I decided to limit the crescendos to the really crucial goals and not get over-excited for the rest. In the meantime, my expert summariser would help me keep up with play, explain the nuances and try to inform a new audience while entertaining them at the same time. I have to admit I got more of a buzz from the professional challenge than the game itself and was delighted to hear that this minority sport, appearing on a minority channel, was pulling in regular audiences of over 100,000.

Amidst all this, there was a rather more significant moment in television history when Jacqui Oatley became the first female commentator on *Match of the Day*. I had to laugh when Simon Jordan, the flamboyant former chairman of Crystal Palace, was among those who howled with derision. 'Ridiculous,' he said. 'After all, you wouldn't expect to find a man commentating on netball.' Simon was obviously not among our viewers on Sky! I shared a joke with Jacqui along those lines and I sympathised with her because the reaction was just hysterical. I happen to have known her from before she entered broadcasting because, as part of her media training, she joined me for a game at Hillsborough which I was covering for 5 Live. She struck me then as a bright girl and I was delighted to help her with her university thesis. Like a good many others, Jacqui has now left me standing. But it would be nice to think that, between us, we have helped break down some old taboos.

For all that, I couldn't take myself too seriously as a netball commentator. Eventually England Netball, a major stakeholder in the Sky project, decided they wanted more of a shouting style of commentator which I didn't think was right for the sport. It wouldn't have been a surprise to have been replaced in my early fumbling weeks but by the end of the second season I felt I'd got it well and truly cracked, as the audience figures seemed to reflect. Yet, on reflection, I feel two years was long enough. I look back with pride on this pleasant diversion in my career and with gratitude to Televideo, who had previously commissioned me to front a series of behind-the-scenes videos on clubs including Manchester City, Leeds, Sheffield Wednesday and Hull City in the 1980s.

Golf is one sport I've hardly ever played and never reported on—fortunately. But I am not quite the total ignoramus who approached Sam Torrance for an interview during a practice round for the British Masters at Woburn where I had been sent purely to busk a few preview interviews for independent radio in 1985. Sam was out on the course when I asked him to talk but he was amenable enough and suggested we chat on the move.

We were on the fairway at the time, which is an important detail. Ridiculously, I blew my pretence at knowing something about golf by saying: 'Sam Torrance, here we are walking on the green at Woburn . . . what about your chances tomorrow?' Sam simply increased his stride and marched on leaving me in his wake. In case you're wondering, I *do* know the difference between the green and the fairway. But Sam obviously thought I didn't and wasn't prepared to make allowances for my silly slip. Later that day, I interviewed another golfing great who, in 1971, became the first player to win the US, Canadian and British Open in the same year. I also hit on the magic formula, explaining to Lee Trevino that I knew absolutely nothing about the sport and had been dropped right in it. Trevino, a great talker at any time, chatted away for about 10 minutes non-stop and it was mesmerising stuff. There are times when the old saying is true; ignorance can be bliss.

12

THRILLS AND SPILLS

There are times when you think you've seen it all. Thankfully you never have. From a star player pushing a referee to the ground to a Premier League manager berating his players on the pitch at half-time and a beach ball 'scoring' a goal in a top game, I've been on the spot for some pretty amazing events. And the beauty of the job is that you never know when or where the next unprecedented drama will unfold. The only certainty is that it will.

It's these events rather than great victories and brilliant goals that imprint themselves most vividly on your mind. But first I'll take you back to the results from two matches on successive nights in 1978 . . . Sheffield United 1 Liverpool 0 and Rotherham United 3 Arsenal 1. These were two massive shocks in the League Cup and I was lucky enough to be behind the microphone for both. I remember the goals quite clearly . . . Gary Hamson for the Blades against the mighty Merseysiders and Dave Gwyther, John Green and Richard Finney for the less than mighty but (on that night) magnificent Millers. Never before or since have I known such a sequence of shock results in South Yorkshire.

Something else happened around that time and it had nothing to do with the actual football. I can't even remember the game, only that it was a night match at Saltergate, home of Chesterfield FC, and that it almost became my home for the night. First, let me explain that Saltergate has always been my theatre of dreams. When my family moved north to Chesterfield from Kent in 1963, the Spireites were quick to claim my affections. I was just getting interested in football at the time and the local club represented a safer environment than nearby Bramall Lane or Hillsborough, although my dad did take me to the odd game in Sheffield.

My heroes were the boys in blue, especially the Fourth Division promotion team of 1969–70. Players like Ernie Moss, Kevin Randall, Tom Fenoughty and John Archer were gods to me. It was around that time that I took up the hobby of writing my own match reports, little realising where this would lead. Then, at 17, I even approached the club about writing a yearbook. It never got off the ground but the idea caught the attention of BBC Radio Sheffield and for the first time I hit the airwaves, interviewed by sports editor Mike Marsh. The thrill of hearing yourself on the radio, much like the first time you see your name in print, was indescribable. I was painfully shy and yet my love of sport and ability in English was a way of expressing myself. So it was that I would write to the 'Tell it to Tony' letters page in the Saturday night *Green 'Un* sports paper. Tony was Tony Hardisty. When he moved on to the national scene, Tony Pritchett took over for a seamless transition. These two writers were also heroes of mine and I could scarcely imagine that I would get to know both of them very well as helpful senior colleagues.

Fast forward to that night game at Saltergate in the era of Arthur Cox. He was a no-nonsense character but he agreed, sometime after the game, to come up to the press box for a radio interview. There were only the two of us in the stand. When we'd finished, Arthur scurried back to the offices below leaving me to pack away my equipment. I came down the stairs to the narrow concourse only to discover that the connecting door to the club's offices was closed tight. Evidently Arthur had locked it behind him, maybe thinking I would exit some other way. But the main gates in the turnstile area were also locked.

It was pitch dark and as I groped my way down the corridor I realised there was no way out. All I had for company was the paper cups that rustled in the breeze blowing through the stand.

Saltergate was a spiritual home for me—but this was a little too close to the real thing. It was spooky, to say the least. There were no mobiles in those days, of course, but my saving grace proved to be the one telephone still connected in the press box.

Even then, my escape was complicated. From memory, I had to dredge up the club's switchboard number. I tried it repeatedly but it was either engaged or just ringing out. There was only one thing for it. I rang Chesterfield's police headquarters, via directory enquires, and about 20 minutes later (only just ahead of closing time as I was badly in need of a pint!), I was released by a rather agitated Arthur Sutherland, the club secretary. There was no apology, it was as if I was putting him out. But the incident did at least give me an interesting story to tell and it made a front page side column in Sheffield's *Morning Telegraph* the next day.

I'm sure Cox had a laugh about it, too, because the so-called 'Ayatollah' was not without a sense of humour. Mostly, though, he was a little frightening, as his players would testify. He would click his heels and everyone would stand to attention. The other side to him came out at my expense—again—when I was invited to a dressing room drinks reception to mark a car sponsorship deal for the players. Champagne was flowing and in an era when I was foolishly dismissive of the drink-drive laws, I indulged myself heartily.

Arthur obviously spotted that my glass was always full. It transpired that he quietly arranged to have one of the empty champagne bottles filled with water. From this he poured me another drink when I'd drained the contents of my latest glass. I'd had so much that I carried on drinking without noticing that the liquid had undergone a dramatic change in nature. Arthur lapped it up.

Another thing. If you ever come to shake hands with Arthur, brace yourself and fix your grin even if it becomes more of a grimace. His iron grip is a bone-cruncher, the hardest handshake in football. By the way, the most bizarre food-and-drink episode I've experienced was in the company of Alan Woodward, a brilliant player alongside Tony Currie for Sheffield United in the Seventies. We were at the bar at the Owlerton Stadium dog track and Woody suddenly challenged me to eat a cream cracker biscuit in less than a minute. How that came into the conversation, I've no idea. Playing along, I took him up on it, thinking the task was easy, and there was a pint on it as I recall. He got the drink but I needed it more than him because I ended up with a mouthful of 'cardboard' that I just couldn't swallow. Well, not in the time allotted. You try it. And this wasn't the first or last time I have bitten off more than I can chew.

Another Arthur Cox story before we move on. This one proves that it wasn't only trembling players and journalists who were frightened of him. Astonishing though it may still seem, Chesterfield were the biggest spenders in the country on transfer deadline day in 1980. They shelled out around £250,000 on three players which, for a club with a previous record outlay of some £20,000, was truly astonishing. I felt that the most relevant interview would be with the chairman rather than the manager, so I contacted local builder Ian Gaunt who fronted the board at that time. He was not wildly keen but agreed a time and place to meet.

As a courtesy, I mentioned this to Cox and he was furious. 'Don't you go speaking to my chairman,' he said. I'm proud to say I stuck to my guns because on this occasion I was a little too angry on my own account to be afraid. I told Arthur I would be interviewing his chairman as arranged and held that position even when he said something like 'in that case, you won't be talking to me again'. I was fuming when I came off the phone. Managers can't tell you not to talk to their boss. This was outrageous. A little while later, my phone rang. It was a rather mealy-mouthed Ian Gaunt telling me that, on second thoughts, he'd rather not do the interview. Arthur had obviously got to him and I was more than a little annoyed. That tells you something about the power Cox wielded, even though it was the board who had put up the money for him to spend. I doubt even Sir Alex Ferguson could have pulled that one off.

My good friend, Nigel Dean, a former radio colleague now doing very well for himself at Sky, clearly misjudged my relationship with Arthur when he went to work for BBC Radio Derby at a time when Cox was in charge of the Rams. By way of introduction, Nigel somehow thought it would gain favour to say he had worked with me. 'Eh, that's no recommendation!' retorted Arthur.

One game I recall for one incident rather than the score was between Sheffield United and Liverpool in the early Nineties. Bruce Grobbelaar was Liverpool's brilliant but sometimes eccentric goalkeeper and that day he had one of his moments of madness, rashly racing from his goal and stranding himself halfway down one touchline as Brian Deane adroitly chipped into an empty net.

I had enjoyed a previous chance meeting with Bruce. We were both with our families on a holiday flight to South Africa in 1989 just days after Liverpool had surrendered the title by losing 2–0 at home to Arsenal. During a stopover at Johannesburg en route for Durban, a young child came toddling out of first class and encountered my own 20-month old son in the aisle. Grobbelaar then magically appeared in pursuit of his kid right in front of me. We had an impromptu chat, something about the weather and a guarded comment from me about how Arsenal had stolen the title. He was friendly. I didn't tell him I was a journalist—what a conversation-stopper that would have been!

But our next meeting was different. I steeled myself to approach Grobbelaar in the dressing room corridor after his Bramall Lane gaffe. 'Yes,' he said in a loud intimidating tone as he thrust his head right into mine and fixed me with a threatening stare. He was defying me to ask him about his blunder. I did all the same, albeit a little half-heartedly. 'About the goal,' I said.

'Which goal and what about it?' he barked.

'Er, the one where you came out,' I ventured.

'It was a mistake, a mistake,' he rapped, as if I was a fool for asking the obvious, and then he strode off. Some years later, Bruce came to Sheffield Wednesday for a short spell at the end of his career and could not have been more charming. I don't suppose he would remember any of the three meetings or make a connection, but he was certainly an interesting character to meet.

There was no confrontation for me in September 1998 but I was faced with the most startling incident I have ever seen on a football field. This was the day at Hillsborough when Paolo Di Canio, the Italian star playing for Sheffield Wednesday, pushed a referee to the ground. Actually, that statement is open to debate because the official in question, Paul Alcock, has been variously accused since then of 'taking a dive' by falling backwards. It was certainly a comical tumble when you look at the replays but, at the time, with the naked eye, the vision was clear . . . Di Canio shoved the referee in the chest and effectively pushed him over.

I was reporting the game on 5 Live and I wish I had a pound for every time in the ensuing weeks that they used a clip of my instant reaction in trailers for the Saturday show. 'This is sensational. Paolo Di Canio, having just been sent off, has pushed the referee to the ground . . .' It happened right in front of me on the touchline nearest the press box. And it happened as if in slow motion. I was already geared to go live to report Di Canio's sending off. The game was being filmed for *Match of the Day*, so the studio boys had the pictures and they came to me straight after Alcock hit the deck. You don't have time to think in moments like those, you just use instinct and describe what you are seeing. The problem was that all hell was breaking loose and you had to split your brain to rewind the complicated sequence that led to this extraordinary flashpoint.

An initial clash between Wednesday's Petter Rudi and Arsenal's Patrick Vieira sparked a confrontation between Di Canio and Martin Keown. The Italian was called over to be shown the red card by Alcock and the rest is history. But it doesn't necessarily record that Di Canio and Nigel Winterburn then had a set-to on the touchline. It was absolute mayhem! So much was going off, including Wednesday manager Danny Wilson having an apologetic word with the referee, that somehow I failed to notice that Keown had also been sent off. The studio handed straight back to check and I had to be vague, saying presumably he had been red-carded as he wasn't on the field.

'Well, I doubt he's gone off to go the toilet,' piped up Alan Green when the afternoon's main match commentary was resumed. Colleagues of Greeny, who's a very entertaining broadcaster and has always been friendly with me, would say that was a typically sarcastic comment. I doubt he means to offend, but he's certainly not conspicuous for rushing to the aid of colleagues in trouble and his quips can be unnecessarily barbed. He, of course, would have had the back-up of a co-commentator and producer. I was on my own. At half-time, I did a round robin of other broadcasters and was relieved to discover that no-one, but no-one, had noticed Keown being shown the red card. There was too much going on and he had simply slipped off the pitch unnoticed.

Di Canio was banned for a total of 11 matches while Alcock claimed the incident had aggravated a back injury. He did seem to go down easily but there was no doubt he was shoved and the Italian deserved his punishment. Wednesday boss Wilson suddenly had a legitimate reason to show Di Canio the door and the club gladly accepted a £1.2m cheque from West Ham. The move resurrected his career and Paolo was bound for Manchester United when I secured the first interview with Alcock, as he reflected on what had occurred more than three years earlier.

He urged Sir Alex Ferguson to complete the signing of a gifted player who had previously given him no trouble, but there was still a hint of bitterness and irony. I quote Alcock from my article in the *Daily Mail* of 4th January 2002: 'I'm so pleased I revitalised his career and I wish I had been on 10% of everything he has earned since. He was basically unrecognised at the time of the incident and I think it set him alight. You can never predict anything like what happened at Hillsborough. I certainly didn't expect it and I don't think he expected to be doing it. He's an excitable chap but I wouldn't think he will contemplate doing anything like it again.'

You could easily transfer many of those words and apply them to the former Hull City manager, Phil Brown, based on his extraordinary behaviour at Manchester City on Boxing Day, 2008. I was there to see him sit his players down on the pitch at half-time and remonstrate with them angrily. Or *not* see it as the case may be. This was an incident that caught me entirely on the hop during my coverage of the game for BBC television's *Final Score*.

To give you an insight, City were leading 4–0 approaching the break, at which point I was intently scribbling a 30-second half-time report. When you cover Premiership games for the programme, they hand to you almost instantly when the whistle blows because they have the benefit of a live feed of the pictures. So at that point it's head down looking at your notebook as you gallop through a summary in the time allotted. I was approaching my final sentence when the voice of editor Stephen Booth broke through on my headphones, saying: 'Talk about the Hull players on the pitch— we've got pictures.' What players on the pitch?

This was a classic pantomime moment along the lines of 'he's behind you'. Well, 'he's in front of you' might have been more appropriate. It was only at this moment that I lifted my head to see Hull's players squatting in a semi-circle in the far corner of Eastlands right in front of the visiting fans. I was a long way from it and did my best to describe a scene which I didn't fully comprehend. Neither did anybody else. In the studio, presenter Ray Stubbs and various pundits couldn't understand Brown's thinking in staging such a public rebuke of his players who were kept out on the pitch on what was a freezing cold day.

By chance, I had been out drinking with Phil in the company of a few journalistic pals just a fortnight earlier. He had come to a Christmas managers' lunch in Sheffield and really gave the ball a kick. Maybe he enjoyed himself a bit too much! Phil came across as a real extrovert character and we thoroughly enjoyed his banter. It was definitely in his nature to do something that was intended to shock and he defended his actions, even though Hull went into freefall after an excellent start to their first season in the top flight and only just avoided the drop. Brown was accused of losing the respect of his players and many of them were definitely affronted by the events of that Boxing Day. But for me and everyone else present, it was another first. The clear lesson for me was to always expect the unexpected. And now, whenever the half-time whistle blows, I try to keep an eye on the pitch and never assume the players will just walk off with the referee.

Something else I will never again count on is that a stray balloon blowing onto the pitch won't play a crucial part in the action. I refer to Sunderland's 'beach ball goal' against Liverpool on 17th October 2009. As *Final Score*'s man at the Stadium of Light, I had barely noticed what I at first considered to be a red balloon wafting onto the pitch from the Liverpool end. The ball that mattered was in the opposite penalty area at the time, but Sunderland broke at speed for Darren Bent to score with a fierce low shot that appeared to ricochet into the net as it sped through a line of players in front of Liverpool keeper Pepe Reina.

When presenter Mark Chapman handed to me straight after the net had bulged, I put it down to a normal deflection off a defender and said as much, without referring to the stray balloon. But I did mention an ongoing protest from Reina, saying I couldn't understand it as no-one appeared to be offside. Mark and the pundits were equally puzzled. 'We'll have a look at that one again but first let's head off to another game,' he said. When the studio boys picked up they came to a conclusion that couldn't have left me more surprised if they'd announced that aliens had landed in the car park. Bent's shot had deflected in off the beach ball, completely wrong-footing Reina—who went for the wrong ball!

I felt guilty for not spotting it but a quick check around colleagues in the press box confirmed that they were also none the wiser. In fact, I had to tell them what I'd heard and they were equally astonished. This was early in the game and the other problem was knowing that from this point, across numerous live updates, I would have to refer to the incident every single time and have to come up with a variety of different ways of describing it. I was in shock for a good 10 minutes but pulled myself together to count my blessings for being there. It was the talk of the day.

But the debate didn't end on Saturday night. At the time, I assumed—as did everyone else, it seemed—that referee Mike Jones was right to award the goal on the basis that it was just a freak incident not covered in the rules. Wrong. Some anoraks discovered that the beach ball was an 'outside agent' interfering in play and the goal should have been disallowed. Yet Jones and the linesman concerned had no more hope of seeing what really happened than the rest of us. Some reports inferred that they had cocked up by not knowing the rules. Wrong again. They just hadn't seen it. At a service station off the A19 on the way back from the North East, I bumped into Guy Mowbray, who had been the *Match of the Day* commentator for the game. With a higher view halfway up the stand, Guy said he had guessed that the beach ball was involved somehow. But he confessed that, like the rest of us, he made the wrong call on whether the goal should have stood.

Yes, it's always the quirky incidents that leave the biggest impression on those charged with calling games. I must have run over a Black Cat—literally—because another awkward incident befell me at the Stadium of Light two months later. This was the commentator's nightmare of scorer identification. Sunderland were leading 1–0 in stoppage time against Portsmouth who had forced a corner. I was hastily preparing a live full-time report while still watching the action. The corner came in low and pinballed into the net . . . off somebody. I didn't know who.

Worse, the goalscorer stripped off his shirt and disappeared into the Pompey fans behind the goal to celebrate wildly. A sharp-eyed pundit back in the studio rescued me as I played for time in my instant description of the goal and the saviour words floated into my headphones: 'Younes Kaboul.' A good job, too, as I realised Kaboul had already been booked and a second yellow card for taking his shirt off would signal a red. Going live with that drama also meant that I had to ad-lib my full-time report which was delivered barely a minute later. But that's what we do it for, the excitement and adrenaline which provides the stimulus to see you through. And, yes, it really is a drug. As one hooked user, I live for many more moments like this.

Highlighting these freakish events is no disrespect to the many great players and games I've seen. None greater than Tony Currie. His Bramall Lane peak came before I started in the job but I vividly remember watching from the terraces with my Arsenal-supporting dad as TC magically orchestrated a 5–0 victory over the Gunners in 1973. This was sweet revenge for Arsenal winning by the same score at the Lane the previous season when Alan Ball famously sat on the ball. Tony, ever the showman, did the same. And I was there, too, when Currie scored his 'quality goal by a quality player'—to borrow John Motson's memorable line of commentary—to clinch a 3–2 win over West Ham. The tannoy man also summed it up neatly with his choice of record as the players came off—Limmie and Family Cooking's *You can do magic*. It was all about one man and quite rightly so.

Currie was a god to me when I began covering football for Sheffield Cablevision in 1975. There were rampant rumours of a big money transfer—he eventually moved to Leeds the following year—and he was such a star that I was sent to 'doorstep' him at his home in Sheffield on one occasion. This was the first time I actually met him. Not the ideal introduction. Here I was knocking on his door unannounced. But Tony didn't seem to mind this intrusion on his privacy and politely answered questions about his future. By contrast with his flamboyant style on the pitch, blond hair flowing and shirt outside shorts, Tony's actually quite a reserved character. There's no side to him and he remains a popular guy around the club as the perfect ambassador for Sheffield United.

Chris Waddle's masterclass in a 5–0 demolition of West Ham by Sheffield Wednesday during the 1993–94 season also stands out as perhaps the finest individual performance I've seen, only matched by Juninho's wizardry for Middlesbrough a few years later. Geography plays a part and I have been limited by lack of success in my part of the world. But Sheffield Wednesday's 2–1 FA Cup semi-final win over Sheffield United — Waddle again — was memorable and so was Sheffield United's run to two semi-finals, plus the play-off final, under Neil Warnock in 2003.

But the die was cast in our household. I've always been strictly neutral in covering the Sheffield teams, using my support of Chesterfield against all those people who swear blind that I favour one team over the other. In truth, I want both the Blades and the Owls to do well. Not only is it in my best interests but I have developed a genuine affection for both clubs and I try to present them in a good light where possible.

But I will make this confession. In 1993, aged five, my son, Ashley, asked me which team he should follow. At the time, there was only one choice: Wednesday. They've been on the slide almost from that day forward and Ash has blamed me ever since, while, to his great credit, remaining loyal to the Owls.

Memories include watching Barnsley bring the Premier League big boys to Oakwell, but there were also some fun moments outside my patch. The reason I recall Paul Sturrock's Plymouth side clinching one of their promotions in a night match at Rochdale was for what happened afterwards. Manager and players escaped the travelling Pilgrims who swarmed onto the pitch and they reappeared at the back of the tiny main stand immediately behind the press box. They proceeded to uncork numerous bottles of champagne and spray them into the air. A good deal of the fizzy stuff went all over my back and I also had a champagne shampoo without consuming a single drop. On the way home, I prayed for the police to stop my car and sniff me out with breathalyser at the ready. No luck. Where are the police when you really want them?

By far the most dramatic end-of-season game I ever covered was at Scarborough on 8th May 1999 . . . even though the main drama was elsewhere. It doesn't get more emotionally powerful than a club being relegated from the Football League. That's what happened to Scarborough that day. And yet it will always be remembered for the events that unfolded 100 miles away. I was 5 Live's reporter at the McCain stadium on the North Yorkshire coast, hoping—as you always do on these occasions—for a notable escape by the home team. Peter Slater, across at Brunton Park in Carlisle, will have been wishing for the same. He must have prayed harder than me on the Friday night!

Peter ended up with the story of his dreams while I was plunged into nightmare territory. For anyone who doesn't remember, this is what happened. Scarborough thought they were safe after drawing 1–1 with Peterborough but the Carlisle game was still in progress— and goalkeeper Jimmy Glass went up for a late corner to score a 95th minute winner against Plymouth that will stay in football folklore for all time.

Let me explain that as a national radio reporter you become incredibly close to the action in circumstances like this. I knew full well that Carlisle fans had my Scarborough updates pressed to their ears and Peter will have been acutely aware of the same. You had to pinch yourself—particularly at the bigger grounds with large crowds—when the programme switched from your live news of an important goal to the grounds of other clubs affected by it. There would be a tidal wave of reaction from the crowd based on the news you had just imparted. Power, eh? But only when you got it right, which added to the tension.

It was against this backdrop that Peter and myself were having our own professional palpitations. And it became particularly personal for me when Scarborough finished at 1–1. As things stood, a point was enough for safety and many home fans celebrated on the pitch. But the older, wiser ones around the press box kept looking to me for confirmation of full-time at Carlisle. That didn't happen for several minutes—and only after the incredible news from Peter that Carlisle's goalkeeper, of all people, had scored the late, late winner.

I had to tell people around me in hushed tones more befitting of a bereavement. But I had to quickly shut myself off from their grief—and yes, that's not too strong a word when a football club effectively dies—because the outcome of the survival cliffhanger was the top news on *Sports Report* at five o'clock. Presenting a considered view so quickly was one of the most difficult undertakings of my career. *Sports Report* pieces were much longer in those days—around 50 seconds—and had to be crafted with care. The bare detail wasn't sufficient and normally you had just enough time to sculpt your words. On this occasion I simply had to busk it, and Peter was in the same boat.

I must say that, sad as I was for Scarborough, I didn't begrudge his top billing on that story. I remain indebted to Peter for my big breakthrough in broadcasting. After I went freelance in 1985, I concentrated on newspapers while keeping my radio hand in with a Sunday morning breakfast show on Hallam called *Bacon and Biggs*. Corny or what? You can tell I liked deejaying. Incidentally, I was proud as punch when programme boss Keith Skues told me I had the highest audience of the week with nearly 120,000 tuning in.

I loved doing that show but shifted direction after doing a spot of timekilling in my car having parked up for a match somewhere. I located the local radio station and heard what passed for pre-match previews from fans with microphones who sounded like they were reporting from the terraces. If I can't do better than that I'm the Pope, I thought. So, heading back that night, I resolved to ring Radio Sheffield's sports editor Robert Jackson to see if I could do the odd match for him whenever I was at a local game for *Today* newspaper.

Bob was brilliant and invited me on board. It meant I had to give up my show on the rival commercial station and that was hard. But just being on the BBC was like stepping onto a magic carpet. Within weeks I heard that national BBC radio (who then broadcast sport on Radio Two) were in the hunt for a northern football reporter. Peter Slater, who I'd got to know while he was working at Metro in Newcastle, very kindly recommended me and I did a trial match for Radio Two when Sheffield Wednesday played Spurs at Hillsborough. I was such an unknown quantity to them that I was introduced as 'Alan Gibbs'. But they liked the report, which was all that mattered. And they'd learned my name by the next time.

One unforgettable match among many was Bobby Robson's first home game in charge of his beloved Newcastle United in September 1999. I was on duty for both radio and television via the Sunday *Grandstand* programme who often required 5 Live's reporter to double up. What a story unfolded as Newcastle steamrollered Sheffield Wednesday 8–0 with Alan Shearer grabbing five of them. Bobby couldn't have dreamt it better.

But the St James' Park occasion I most vividly recall from this era was the night England tried to bring back Robson as national team manager. I found myself at the centre of the story in covering Newcastle's game that day. It is a somewhat less than lucrative venue for me . . . as per usual on trips to the North East, I had dropped off my family at the Metro Centre where I imagine my match fee disappears very rapidly. I'd arranged to pick them up soon after the game en route for a week's break in the Lake District. But, of course, I was otherwise engaged—and what I most remember is my wife ringing my mobile to see where I was while I was giving a live update to Richard Littlejohn on 606. He thought it was a scream. I was finally cleared to leave the ground at about 6.30, but clearly nobody told Richard. We listened to the rest of his show on the way to the Lakes and it was comical to hear him say 'We'll be going back to Alan Biggs at Newcastle just as soon as we have any more news'. Oh, no you won't.

My final match memories are games when I wasn't working. In 1997, I rediscovered what it was like to be a fan amid Chesterfield's sensational run to the FA Cup semi-finals. Freelances tend to fall by the wayside when the really big games come around, but this had an upside for me as I took Ash to Saltergate for the quarter-final with Wrexham. You become institutionalised in press boxes and forget how to cheer. But I was jerked back to life that day as Chris Beaumont lobbed the winner for a momentous 1–0 win. Here's a further admission; I went all soppy that day. I tend not to get over-emotional at matches, even when I'm shouting down microphones, but that afternoon I cried. I really cried. Tears flowed at the final whistle as I tried to comprehend how my little team, in the lower divisions all my life, were suddenly one step from Wembley. It was all too much.

For the semi with Middlesbrough at Old Trafford, I took Ash again. This time *he* cried. There's no helping us! Chesterfield won a penalty to go 2–0 up. Sean Dyche blasted it home and pandemonium broke out. I bearhugged a big bloke in front and another chap's glasses fell off. He couldn't have cared less and, in all the commotion, didn't even bother searching for them. That's the sort of mania that overtakes the football supporter in these special moments. Later, of course, it was Chesterfield manager John Duncan's glasses that flew off as he celebrated Jamie Hewitt's late extra-time equaliser for a 3–3 draw. This was after Boro had brought tears to my son's eyes by storming from behind with 10 men.

But I kept a stiff upper lip because somehow I had suspected as much. The feeling as Dyche stepped up to take the spot-kick was that if this went in, Chesterfield were in the final. Once the celebrations subsided, everyone seemed to look at their watch. There were some 30 minutes remaining—a long time against the Juninhos and Ravanellis of this world. Then again, Jonathan Howard would have made it 3–1 at one point had not referee David Elleray failed to spot that the ball went over the line.

I was almost alone among Blues fans for having some sympathy with Elleray for copping out. We were sitting level with the goal at that end and the whole thing happened so fast that it was impossible to tell with the naked eye. That's something we all tend to forget, relying on replays for our infinite wisdom. Anyway, it was all a wonderful achievement by the club. In the circumstances, I liked the humour former Chesterfield council leader Bill Flanagan applied to the incident at an event to celebrate the team's achievement. 'I'd like to award Mr Elleray the freedom of the borough,' he said. 'Middlesbrough!'

13

BIGGSY'S BALLS-UPS

These are mistakes you dread at the time but which then become a delight. Well, mostly. There are some I've made that embarrass me still and I'll be as honest as I can about those. But in the main any broadcasting career is the poorer for not having a good smattering of those cringeworthy gaffes that confirm your membership of the hapless human race. The trick is not to have too many—and to have them well spaced out—or you won't have much of a career to relay.

Where I fell foul of that golden rule in both categories was during an early news assignment for Radio Hallam covering parts of Her Majesty the Queen's visit to South Yorkshire and North Derbyshire during her silver jubilee year of 1977. I was whispering into a live microphone on the steps of Chesterfield town hall as Her Majesty passed within a few feet of me on her way in for a civic reception. Actually, I was close enough to have leaned over for a chat had it not been for the warning, on pain of death, not to approach the royal personage. Actually, it's a good job that I was talking quietly enough to have remained just out of earshot. To my horror, I was told later by the council leader, Bill Flanagan, who would regularly join our band of guzzling journalists around town, that I described the Queen as 'probably the most famous person ever to have visited Chesterfield'. Worse still, I apparently remarked that she seemed to be wearing the same turquoise outfit she had donned in Sheffield the day before. As if. Bill laughed his head off at my ignorance in these matters.

There was also an uncomfortable moment when I covered, along with Roger Moffat, the Queen's appearance at a marquee reception in Sheffield's Hillsborough Park. The combination was a recipe for disaster. Roger was renowned for foot-in-mouth disease, having been sacked by the BBC for broadcasting a hoax gale warning, and he also had another affliction involving his mouth where alcoholic beverages were concerned. But he was a confirmed royalist and needed no persuading to stay on the wagon on this occasion. Assisting him was a green, gauche young reporter with little understanding of royal etiquette. As I say, a recipe for disaster.

The other problem was that, for security reasons, we were locked in an empty Hillsborough Park for hours before the Queen's arrival. Breaking the boredom, Roger impishly suggested we enter the big tent marked ER. Once inside, we went through all the cabinets of a huge reception desk. All empty—but so much for security. Shortly afterwards, we both had to go live for a chat together by way of a colour piece anticipating the event and I could not resist remarking: 'You've been going through the Queen's drawers, haven't you Roger?' In any other circumstances, Keith Skues, anchoring the show back in the studio, would have found this funny because he had a great sense of humour, particularly about things going wrong. But on this occasion there was a long uncomfortable silence which nobody dare break with a guffaw. It was very inappropriate and a big learning curve for me.

My news bulletins were another breeding ground for blunders, particularly those in late morning as I was winding down after starting before the crack of dawn. Roger was a witness to one of those during his nine-to-twelve programme. Presenter and newsreader would occupy the same studio. Roger would often appear almost to nod off but even he turned round with a start at my description of a petrol tanker wagon overturning on the M1. 'Petrol' and 'tanker' were pronounced correctly but 'wagon' came out as rhyming with the previous word. Thus a 'petrol tanker wanker overturned on the M1'. A correction barely suffices in circumstances like that.

And there was also the time, relaying a scrap metal theft, that I reported that a ton of 'crap metal' had been stolen.

Things barely improved when I moved on to sport. Here I had John McEnroe winning 'in straight sex'. You couldn't make it up. At other times, I would make an ass of myself by trying to contrive something funny. We had a reporter at a Rotherham away match called Richard Whittington, which was a name to conjure with. When I came to him once I said: 'It's your turn again Dick Whittington . . .' I couldn't resist. He left a pretty disgusted pause and just carried on as normal because he must have heard this supposed joke more than a few times before in his life. In much the same way, young sub-editors on papers think it's clever when they come up with the headline: 'Blunt Blades.' But the funniest editorial story I've ever heard concerned a *Sheffield Star* worker, new to the area, who was compiling a local cricket round-up. Now there happens to be a village near Worksop called Rhodesia and they had a team in the league. When the young sub came to the name, Rhodesia, he frowned and, doffing his cap to political correctness, changed it to Zimbabwe!

There is also a story, absolutely true, of a court reporter for the *Derbyshire Times* who was writing up a case involving a petty local criminal called Ron Powell. Somebody told him, trying to be helpful, that Powell was the former Chesterfield goalkeeper. Well, Chesterfield did indeed have a keeper called Ron Powell back in the Fifties and Sixties. But, unknown to the writer who should have checked, this wasn't the same guy. So he wrote an introduction along the lines of . . . 'Ron Powell saved a few in his time but the former Chesterfield goalkeeper couldn't prevent a fine in court this week.' Which would have been very good in other circumstances.

The strange sequel to the tale came when the paper had a predictably indignant complaint . . . except that it came from the Ron Powell who had appeared in court. 'I'm not the former Chesterfield goalkeeper,' he protested bitterly. It turned out that the other Ron Powell was living in retirement outside the area and had to be contacted to be told how his name had been blackened. Glad I wasn't involved in that conversation.

However, I was very much in the firing line during one sports phone-in. I have already described my problems with swearing (not me, the listeners!) but the caller on this occasion was entirely reasonable—at first. He wanted to take issue with the service we provided and in particular the fact that we didn't broadcast a full reading of racing results through the afternoon. I explained that normally we did but sometimes there were so many meetings that we didn't have the time to accommodate them all and we had to be selective. He wasn't satisfied and persisted with complaining about all manner of things. When his tone became tiresome, I'd had enough. 'Just go and read a newspaper then,' I told him. There was a long silence and then he simply said: 'I'm blind.' Get out of that one. Whatever I said, I was too flustered to make a convincing escape.

Another phone-in flap occurred when Keith Hackett, the Sheffield-based former FIFA referee and later boss of England's match officials, joined me in the studio. Keith was on the way up the refereeing ladder at the time. We formed a good relationship and have been friends ever since. In fact, he gave me a rare glimpse into his world by inviting me into the dressing room for an interview before he took charge of the 1979 FA Cup semi-final at Hillsborough. He was always very much in favour of removing refereeing's image as a sort of secret society, a need which is often ignored by those who run the game. But these were more relaxed times and he willingly answered callers' queries with no fear of retribution. This was to be my lot instead. One caller, called Sid, made what I thought was such a ridiculous statement that I told him so and was about to cut him off when Keith interjected: 'Sid's right, that's a very good point.' Naturally, I had to back down and bow to the expert. These days, I tend to think before I speak but Keith often chides me about the revenge of 'Hissing Sid'.

Keith wouldn't have been too impressed, either, by a lapse I made many years later while covering a mundane game between Oldham and Port Vale for 5 Live. It was drifting towards a draw as I put together my full-time report. At Boundary Park, we had a pretty inadequate seat on the back row of the stand rather than in the press box and I had a poor view of what seemed like a minor altercation on the touchline late in the game. Nothing relevant transpired as far as I was concerned and I was surprised when, after delivering my live full-time report and recording another for later use, the producer asked me to interview John Rudge, the Vale manager.

'Fair result?' I asked John.

'Yes, it was,' he said. 'But I'd have been happier if we hadn't had Steve Guppy sent off like that.' I was momentarily stunned, totally unaware of any red cards. But, for once, I'm proud of my response.

Thinking on my feet, I simply said: 'Yes, how did you see that?' And John supplied the vital missing information without the need for me to have to admit I was in total ignorance. Later, I asked the producer if I could do another version of my recorded piece—but didn't tell him the reason! What had happened was that Guppy had been standing on the side of the pitch, out of my vision, when he had received a second yellow card and simply walked off over the touchline. It taught me a lesson and hurt my professional pride that I hadn't twigged first time.

Even more regrettable was my decision-making on the occasion of Cliff Thorburn's first ever televised 147 snooker break at the Crucible in 1983. I was presenting *Sportacular* in the Hallam studio while Gerry Kersey was our man over the green baize. Gerry was spot on, sensing history in the making early in the break. I should explain that snooker doesn't lend itself to radio commentary so I took a couple of quick updates from Gerry during what was to become a momentous frame. Then I had a problem. Commercial breaks had to go in strict time slots which had to be logged and anyone who failed to hit these had to face the wrath of the station's formidable sales manager Audrey Adams.

It so happened that a break (of the commercial variety) was due just as Thorburn was approaching the colours. Wait and I'd miss the slot. I calculated that we could just squeeze the ads in because Cliff was not known as 'The Grinder' for nothing. It was the worst decision of my sporting life. When I came out of the break to hand back to the Crucible, Gerry was almost drowned out by the rapturous applause, having seen Cliff sink the final black without being able to get on air to describe it. We laugh about it now but I still feel personally sorry for Gerry at having, through no fault of his own, missed commentating on one of the great moments in sport. I should have listened to my better instincts and to hell with the consequences. Rules are there to be broken and this was a time for applying common sense.

Another of our snooker reporters was Peter Jenkins, a schoolteacher who would not only give up his Saturdays to report football but would work late into the night (or even early morning) during the Crucible fortnight. Peter was very knowledgeable and would glean all sorts of behind-the-scenes information whatever the sport. It was as a tribute to his professionalism and the fact that he was a good sport, that we played a prank on him one Saturday afternoon. He knew all things Sheffield United and was at Bramall Lane for a home game. I was in the studio as usual. I arranged with the engineer for the programme, Mick Sylvester, for Peter to receive a fake handover for team news.

How this worked was that, as far as the listeners were aware, I went straight to a record after an ad break. My mike was then taken out of live mode and linked exclusively to Peter's headphones at the ground. He simply heard me give a timecheck out of the break and hand to him for a preview. What I said was this: 'Now let's go to Peter Jenkins at Bramall Lane where a sensational story is breaking. Sheffield United are in talks to sign the Liverpool and Scotland striker Kenny Dalglish. Peter, what's the latest on that?' Of course, this was a total spoof but was still just believable because

United had recently signed another Liverpool legend in Phil Thompson.

Peter must have been absolutely stunned but flannelled his way out of it brilliantly. 'Yes, Alan, the ground here is buzzing with that news etc.' We left him waffling on for the full minute of his preview and only then told him he'd been well and truly had. A cruel joke perhaps, but we knew he could take it.

In hindsight, it was still a rotten trick because it was people like Peter who kept our sports department going. For a pittance of pay, they would give up their Saturdays and weekday nights. So, too, did the former Grimsby manager George Kerr who became a very witty and perceptive matchday summariser. A great character, George. He'd treat you properly and would always get the same in return.

Peter, by the way, will be delighted to learn that a presenter called Lindsay Reed (radio name Michael Lindsay) really had me when I stood in as the presenter of an evening music show. He'd done the previous programme and accidentally on purpose left the studio mike in echo mode. So I got a shock when I introduced the show and heard myself reverberating in my headphones. He'd left the studio by then and was somewhere in the building holding his sides in. I had no idea where the echo switch was located on the desk and had to chase through the corridors to find him while the next record was playing—much to his further amusement.

Lindsay was an impish character. Another time he was 'driving' the desk while I presented *Sportacular* as an outside broadcast from Hillsborough. This meant he played in the records and the ad breaks and opened my mike when I spoke for all the links. We would never play the same record twice, of course. Suddenly in the last hour I heard the Detroit Spinners brilliant hit, 'Working my way back to you', bubbling up underneath me. I carried on regardless and, after talking up to the vocals, waited for Lindsay to close my mike before telling him: 'We've already played this one.' But he hadn't closed the mike in time and the listeners had heard the remark. Knowing that and, perhaps feeling miffed at being chided, he promptly shut down the record . . . leaving me to fill the silence by waffling on about a technical hitch.

Lindsay was primarily an engineer on the station, which explains a lot! They were a fun-loving lot, very likeable as a bunch but a little unstable at times. One of them—I don't know who—still has in his possession a clip of an embarrassing slip I made during a Christmas show. We would take the radio car on the road and turn up to broadcast in back streets or from inside people's houses. This time we were at an old folks home where it was my lot to interview a doddery old couple who'd just been having a game of tiddlywinks. You've guessed it, the last syllable came out all wrong. 'How have you enjoyed your game of tiddlywanks?' Worse still, it was very loud and very clear. Funny thing was that the old folks didn't seem to notice even with hearing aids, but the engineers outside in the van heard all right and they absolutely loved it.

Removing one letter from a word can also have hilarious results. I wondered if it was deliberate after spotting in a local newspaper's weather forecast one day that the letter 'o' was missing from the second word in 'pollen count'. Absolutely true. The revenge of a sub-editor or typesetter on his last day, perhaps? Or maybe the explanation was more innocent because, as journalists, we are all guilty of what we call 'typos'—in the case of words that become mangled somewhere in the process between writer and reader.

Here are two of my favourites. A Derbyshire cricket reporter phoned in a column to Sheffield's *Green 'Un* sports paper in which he referred to the team captain's 'genial exterior.' The copytaker, more often than not a lady with no interest in sport, must have misheard the second word. The captain concerned—a former England batsman called Kim Barnett—was thus reckoned to display 'genial hysteria.' Another time, I was the victim of a subbing error in the *Daily Mail*. Actually, 'victim' is the wrong word because this was a mistake of the type I treasure. I'd written into a match reporter that a Sheffield Wednesday player—who happened to rejoice in the name of Orlando Trustfull—was 'the game's only recipient of a yellow card.' You could remove any one letter and not fall about laughing—except the very last. And so, in the paper, we had Trustfull as the 'recipient of a yellow car' Priceless!

So was another gaffe I recall—because 'priceless' was the exact word Micky Adams was striving for when, as Brighton manager, in an interview on 5 Live, he was discouraging bids for a future England striker called Bobby Zamora. What Micky was trying to say was that no amount of money could buy him. What he actually said was: 'We haven't put a price on Bobby . . . as far as I'm concerned he's absolutely worthless!' Strangely, 'Price' and 'worth' have such similar meaning that Micky unwittingly exposed one of the many vagaries of the English language.

Finally to an episode that is not a blooper as such, more a salient warning to any budding member of my profession. Always believe that the subject of your article will actually read it. Okay, more often than not they won't, much as we like to flatter ourselves that what we write is important. And it's easy to kid yourself that when you are penning a piece for local consumption in, say, Newcastle and make a scathing attack on some chap in Plymouth, that he won't see it and that you can write pretty much what you like. Wrong.

I speak here from uncomfortable experience and, luckily, I learned this lesson early on. Back at the beginning of my freelance career, I had a little column in a free paper called the *Sheffield Gazette*. One week I made some passing remark about the 'schoolmasterly' approach of BBC commentator Barry Davies. Don't know why—I've always enjoyed his measured style, always passionate but never less than precise. Perhaps he had made some remark I didn't agree with or I was simply writing for effect, I can't remember.

At the time, I thought nothing more of it—until, a few days later, the editor of the *Gazette*, a lovely lady called Brenda who happily knew next to nothing about football, phoned me out of the blue to say that a bloke called Barry Davies had been in touch and could I call him back. I laughed and told Brenda: 'Nice try, but I'm not falling for that one.' But she was nonplussed by this and, realising that she had no idea who Barry Davies was, I came to the shock conclusion that the call was genuine.

Noting down Davies's number, I resolved to ring him rather than taking the easy option of ducking out. I'm glad I did. He couldn't have been more magnanimous; he'd simply seen the article having been sent it by a friend and was interested to hear how I had formed my opinion. There was no anger, just curiosity. Faced with this charm offensive, I felt more comfortable about flannelling some unqualified opinion or other before backtracking with gratitude about him taking the trouble to ring me. Barry replied in kind and I came off the phone thinking of him, as I still do, as a really good bloke.

When Davies retired from football commentary after a long and distinguished career in 2004, by which time I at least knew something about the business after many years on 5 Live, I wrote him a congratulatory note. In this, I reminded him of the precocious youngster who had taken issue with him some two decades earlier. When Barry replied by hand a few weeks later, he showed typical grace. In fact, he said he felt the need to make a totally unnecessary apology to me.

Davies wrote: 'Thanks for your letter and my apologies for taking so long to respond. Quite frankly the response to my departure from MOTD has been somewhat overwhelming and you are not the last I need to apologise to.

'I have a hazy recollection of my telephone call, a tactic always interesting and often rewarding, but I have of course heard you often on '5'. You are very generous in your comments and they are very much appreciated.'

Barry Davies was, and is, a class act, as a commentator and as a man. There will always be differences of opinion about who are the best ones. Commentators seem to arouse an emotional response in people—they are loved, liked, tolerated or loathed, depending on an individual's point of view. But I have yet to hear a truly bad one on TV or radio, at least at national level. They all develop their own styles and some of these irritate certain folk. As the saying goes, one man's meat is another's poison. John Motson's passion for statistics might be enjoyed by some viewers and detested by others. But there can be no mistaking that he, like so many, is exceptionally good at his job. It's just that you might prefer one over another.

Finally in this section, the laugh wasn't always on me. Mike Morgan and myself enjoyed one at the expense of our colleagues at a Bramall Lane game in the late 1990s. As was our custom, we used the press box there on the previous day (free phone calls!) to churn out the Friday preview stuff. Suddenly a young couple entered our midst and started a conspiratorial conversation in one corner of the box. Eavesdropping comes easily to journalists and we discovered they were discussing tactics—for a streak across the pitch at the game the following day! Happily, it was only the female who was going to do it—and very fetching she was too. We became silently complicit in her plans and turned up with rather more relish than usual the following day. I teased colleagues with comments like 'I've got this feeling something odd's going to happen today—like a streak or something'. Sure enough, it happened right on cue. 'Told you so' never sounded so good. Our blonde streaker made quite an impression—because I can't say I remember anything else about that game.

14

INSIDER DEALING

I remember how impressed I was early in my career on hearing that Jack Charlton's appointment as Sheffield Wednesday manager had been brokered by David Jones, the then sports editor of the *Morning Telegraph* who was also a broadcaster. David, a lovely bloke who was also helpful to me, had evidently been the go-between on behalf of the club. It meant they knew him as someone of integrity, as did Charlton. So he sat on the story until close to the time it broke. Keith Farnsworth, a colleague who has written several books on Sheffield Wednesday, was another journalist in the inner circle at Hillsborough. Little did I realise that one day I would be entrusted, on several occasions, with that sort of role.

Football is a bit like a village peopled by gossips. The talk is all around and you only have to keep your ears open, while also learning when to keep them closed. I discovered there were two types of off-the-record conversations. There was one not to be repeated to anyone and another for card-marking purposes that could lead to unattributable stories that were often in the teller's best interests as well as your own. The go-between role put you halfway between the two. Your commission would be to be first with the story once the parties involved were agreeable.

I have already mentioned how journalists can be useful tools in the transfer market because of rules preventing players under contract from being approached directly. This also applies to the movement of managers. But everyone in the game knows that there are ways around this stipulation and secret backdoor approaches are made all the time. Anybody who thinks otherwise is completely naïve. Any chairman or manager worth his salt has to play the system because to do otherwise would be to get left behind in this endless game. I mean, Sir Alex Ferguson has been known to pop round for tea with players he has wanted to sign.

Discretion and the fact that the following events were relatively recent prohibits me from mentioning the people involved, but I was phoned by one chairman who was about to sack his manager and told me so. He fancied the manager of a neighbouring club and knew him to be a good contact of mine. Would I make an approach on his behalf? I duly did so and set up a clandestine meeting between the pair outside a hotel on a Sunday afternoon. I was permitted to speculate on the link, with no details given. The parties met but on this occasion things didn't work out. Only a few close friends outside football are privy to the identities involved and one of them, a Sunday night drinking pal called Paul Turner, has repeatedly urged me to spill the beans. But as both the central characters are still in the game it wouldn't be prudent to name names at this point—even though no great crime had been committed. To be honest, it's almost standard procedure.

But I can reveal that I played a small part in Viv Anderson, the first black footballer to play for England, to continue breaking the mould by becoming the manager of Barnsley in the summer of 1993. The former Manchester United defender was playing for Sheffield Wednesday towards the end of his career and I made the initial approach to Viv on behalf of Barnsley's chairman, John Dennis. It was purely a feeler to see if Anderson was interested, which he was. For fear of rejection, clubs prefer to make approaches when they already know the answer.

More commonly, I have often been contacted to recommend would-be managers to certain clubs. It's usually someone you know who fancies a certain job and asks you to put a word in for them on the quiet. Occasionally, they will also encourage you to throw their name into the media speculation game. It's amazing how putting two and two together can add up to four, rather than five. Guesses can become inspired because directors tend not to be particularly clued up on football and will sometimes see a name linked to their club and think: 'That's a good idea.'

In a similar vein I had a call one day from Frank Barlow, a long-time friend and one of the nicest men in football. He was coaching with Birmingham at the time and doing a favour for Steve Bruce, the team's captain who was nearing the end of his time as a player. I didn't know Bruce, who had been a legendary centre-half for Manchester United, but through Frank we spoke on the phone about his interest in Sheffield Wednesday where there was a vacancy after David Pleat was sacked.

I put a word in for Steve but also decided he was a very good shout. It just so happened that my timing was all wrong. I sent the *Daily Mail* a speculative story on Bruce-for-Wednesday not knowing that, around the same time, they were preparing to bring back Ron Atkinson. So I looked a bit sick, to say the least, the next day when my story was overtaken by several papers with the real one. I say next day, but it was actually around midnight of the day I filed on Bruce when the *Mail* rang me with shattering news of what the early editions of rival publications were carrying. I tried to make good my rick by scrambling together a piece for later editions which predicted—correctly as it turned out—that Atkinson was returning as a bridge to landing Danny Wilson the following summer. Although this proved inspired, no amount of backtracking could remove the egg from my face.

But there was a consolation worth having. This was a developing relationship with Steve Bruce who I was in contact with again in the build-up to him being named the manager of Sheffield United. Having 'Brucie' on my patch was a boon. He's a straightforward, honest guy who's very likeable with it and he didn't forget my services rendered. There was no shortage of stories with him at Bramall Lane where, as I recall, I would sometimes have to bring my toddler daughter Isabelle to press conferences. Lynne had gone back to work leaving me holding the baby, but Steve would ensure Izzy was plied with sweets and also take the spice out of his language while the business was being conducted.

I particularly recall how Steve buttonholed me shortly after taking charge to ask about a colleague, the *Star's* veteran writer Tony Pritchett. 'Can I trust him?' said Steve, who wasn't casting aspersions. His enquiry was made because he simply didn't know the man who had the closest day-to-day dealings with the club. I never mentioned any of this to Tony, who is sadly no longer with us. Not the conversation or my answer. 'Yes, you can—he's a good guy who can be trusted,' was my emphatic reply. There was nothing big about this because I feel sure that any of my colleagues would do the same for me, or I hope so anyway. Yes, journalism is a cut-throat business and it did fleetingly cross my mind that praising Tony wouldn't be in my best interests when I had such an opportunity to steal a march on a rival. But I'm glad I supported him—it was the truth, anyway—because pangs of conscience are very bad bedfellows. I try to take the same approach with stories I write, striving to be truthful and honest. They may not always prove to be correct but it's important to have felt they were right at the time.

One of those concerned a Manchester businessman called Mike McDonald when he was the incoming chairman of Sheffield United in 1995. The takeover deal was proving protracted and taking longer than expected. Then I heard from an informed source that the existing directors would bar McDonald from the club, where he was being entertained on matchdays, unless he completed it quickly. Once the story was in the *Daily Express*—where I had moved from the *Mail* for the second of two spells—I rang McDonald for an attempted follow-up. He gave me one alright. He ranted down the phone in a ferocious tirade that included a threat to bar me and ended with him shouting: 'And you can put that in your fucking press.'

Needless to say, the McDonald era at Bramall Lane was not a particularly happy one for me. Or for many others. An essentially friendly club seemed to lose its soul somehow. I have to admit, though, that I took the wrong approach with McDonald at the start; there are two sides to every argument. But Mike and myself managed an arms-length sort of relationship and, although the carpet was suddenly pulled from underneath a good team by the player sales that precipitated his exit, McDonald did have big ideas before making way for Kevin McCabe, easily the best Blades chairman in my time.

McDonald's opening gambit was to install Howard Kendall who had been a huge success in management with Everton. Howard could be an intense character but he had a cracking sense of humour. I referred in a *Sunday Express* match report to his 'hangdog' countenance on the touchline. Around this time there would be a mugshot of me in a rather stern-looking pose accompanying my regular television reports for BBC *Look North*. 'Hangdog!' exploded Howard in his office the following week. 'Have you seen your picture on the telly?' People in glass houses and all that, but this was also Howard having fun.

Even he wasn't having much of that by the time he made an ill-fated return to Goodison and his successor, Nigel Spackman, was moved to quit in mid-season. After a caretaker spell under Steve Thompson and a difficult period with Adrian Heath at the helm of an apparently sinking ship, a new board shored up by Derek Dooley turned to a man who became one of the most successful managers in Sheffield United's modern history.

One's called Neil and the other's called Warnock

Neil is the nice, easy going chap who could turn up at a church fete and charm everyone in sight. Warnock is the raving lunatic who could be coming to a touchline near you. I'd known Neil Warnock for some years before he was appointed Sheffield United manager in 1999. A former Chesterfield and Rotherham player, he'd been bouncing around the non-league scene while also doing a day job as a chiropodist.

It's strange to recall that he once popped into Radio Hallam's reception and asked me to check out if there were any jobs going in the sales department. There weren't, unfortunately. Hallam's loss proved to be football's gain because, if he hadn't become a league manager, Neil would have been a brilliant salesman. He could have sold sand to the Arabs. Neil's just got that gift of the gab and the ability to make people feel at home. But, of course, there are many sides to this colourful character—as referees would be the first to testify. Something happens to Neil between the hours of three and five on a Saturday afternoon that is akin to the transformation between Dr Jekyll and Mr Hyde. A mild-mannered bloke turns into a complete and utter maniac.

How and why is impossible to gauge, except that it's probably because of his sheer passion for football and will to win. That's putting it kindly, perhaps, but I defy anyone who has met Neil in the normal course of events not to like him. He would be as much at home with the ladies of the townswomen's guild as a bunch of players in a dressing room.

In this, he shared some traits with Dave Bassett. Although the Blades' two most successful managers of the modern era are very different people, they both had a keen sense of occasion and an ability to put on different heads. Underneath all Neil's front and bluster, he was intensely serious about the job. What he said publicly during the week (Saturdays apart, you'll notice) was carefully calculated, even some of the more outrageous stuff. He knew how to get under the opposition's skin. And he would brush off with a laugh the rumoured hatred of other managers. Indeed, there were times he would play up to his image and I feel that some of the touchline pantomime is now premeditated because Neil knows what is expected of him as part of the show.

Like Basssett, too, Warnock formed a firm alliance with Derek Dooley. From a media perspective, he liked to be totally in control and was prolific enough with stories to make it unnecessary to hunt out players most of the time. Like most journalists, I found Neil excellent to work with. It went deeper in that he invited my family round for a drink at his harbour-side property in Looe when both of us were on holiday in Cornwall one summer. The following year, we hired out his log cabin in Scotland for a week. Funniest thing there was that the boiler packed up and I had to call in a plumber. There is little coverage of English football in Scotland. Hence the following exchange. Plumber: 'So how do you think you'll do next season?'

Me (hiding my surprise): 'Crap as always.' I was amazed to be mistaken for Neil, which is something that could never happen today! Even in Scotland he would be well recognisable.

What happened shortly afterwards was one of those misunderstandings that can blow up in a journalist's face. Neil, by his own admission, was having a torrid spell of results at one point and knew full well that the consequences would be grave for him if United, after a good start to his reign, didn't pull out of a slump. When I was heading to a match in Lancashire one Saturday, the sports editor of the *Sunday People* rang me for advice. He said he had been sent a story saying that Dave Bassett was likely to return to Bramall Lane in Warnock's place if the club decided to make a change. I didn't want anything to happen to Neil but, in all honesty, I had to tell him it was a good shout since Bassett was already rumoured to be the obvious replacement. Naively, I thought this would be presented in the gossip column as a bit of tittle-tattle with no real damage done because it's the sort of stuff managers are surrounded by all the time. And I couldn't, in truth, knock a logical rumour down. Had I done so, my credibility could have been shot to pieces by subsequent events.

But the next day the story was a huge spread, tagged exclusive and almost presented as fact. Worse still, I was mortified to discover that, from one conversation I hadn't instigated, my name was included as the second bylined writer on the piece. It was as if I was the journalist behind it because the other guy operated from a different area. I couldn't necessarily blame the sports editor because he probably thought that crediting me was doing me a favour, but I should have specified that I didn't want it there—and he later apologised for 'not thinking things through'.

That one cock-up threatened to ruin my relationship with three of my best contacts at a single stroke. Dave wasn't impressed but understood what had happened and advised me to make my peace with Neil and with Derek Dooley, who I was told was particularly upset. Neil was calm but clearly hurt and suggested we take a fortnight's break to let the dust settle. But once Derek and his wife Sylvia, always a good sounding board, had heard the full story of what happened he took my side. 'Fortunately for you,' he said, 'I understand a bit about how newspapers work. And if you say you didn't write that story, then I believe you.' That was typical of Derek and the storm passed.

Even so, I was glad of a chance to make amends and it was amazing how quickly the opportunity presented itself. This was after the so-called Battle of Bramall Lane in March, 2003. Warnock's Sheffield United were 3–0 down to Gary Megson's West Bromwich Albion when the game was abandoned in the second half. Having had three players sent off, the Blades were further reduced by injuries to having only six on the pitch and the referee, Eddie Wolstenholme, had no option but to call a halt under the rules.

All hell broke loose, as if there hadn't been enough on the field. Megson was furious, accusing Warnock of engineering the abandonment, and although the FA subsequently allowed the result to stand, United and their manager were in hot water. Dooley even admitted to me later that he considered resigning as chairman in the aftermath, not least because of his anger with Megson, whose father Don was a long-time friend of Derek's. I could understand Megson's annoyance over the potential loss of three well earned points and he happened to be another good contact from his time as a player with Sheffield Wednesday. But it was a very serious allegation and Neil was personally affronted by it. So was Derek.

I felt the only way Warnock could be completely exonerated was if the referee dismissed a claim which I felt had been made in the heat of the moment, though Megson never retracted it. I had good contacts among match officials and was the only reporter to get hold of Wolstenholme that weekend. He made it clear, on the record, that, as far as he was concerned, there was no attempt made to abandon the match. 'Warnock cleared' was the headline in Monday's *Daily Mail*. Neil, who rang me to hear first hand about this development after I had told Dooley, was clearly grateful and relieved while also feeling vindicated. It was business as usual between us and when United prepared to face the various FA charges that followed from their indiscipline on the field he ensured that I was in the loop on their responses.

Megson, who happens to be a near neighbour of mine, was not so happy. He was distinctly cool when I bumped into him a few weeks later and immediately offered my congratulations on West Brom's subsequent promotion to the Premiership. 'Next time I'm in trouble I know who to come for,' he said by way of a back-handed compliment. I have to say there are two sides to every story and I'm sure I would have tried to assist Gary, who's always been helpful to me, if the roles had been reversed and he had been in charge of one of 'my' clubs. I'm delighted to say that Megson, a very accomplished manager, did join the fold by taking charge of Sheffield Wednesday in February 2011. The reality is that the more connections you have, the more likely you are to be caught in the crossfire. Happily, time is a great healer. Besides, in my job it's more to do with circumstances than taking sides between people you know.

The bottom line is that Warnock proved himself yet again—after having an impact wherever he had been lower down—as a first-class manager. His seven years at Bramall Lane—most of them alongside an excellent coach in Kevin Blackwell, later to return as manager—delivered steady if painstaking progress, a treasured promotion to the Premier League and massive ground redevelopment. He had enormous mental capacity. Once I did an interview in his office while he was rifling through a mountain of paperwork at the same time. He was firmly on top of both tasks. He left Bramall Lane in 2007 after relegation from the top flight when, in hindsight, he would have been the best person to take United back there.

In answer to those who reckon Warnock is off his rocker, I'd have to say that in many ways he's one of the sanest managers I've known. The reason is that he knows how to relax and enjoy himself without relying on football for all his kicks. For one thing, he confesses to being a *Coronation Street* fan (an addiction I share) and he will even delay watching a live game on another channel until after the soap has finished. I've seen him close up with his young family after an invitation for a drink to one of his holiday homes at Looe in Cornwall. Neil couldn't have been further removed from the image of the tensed-up, stressed-out, workaholic modern manager. Granted, he needs to take a sleeping pill before matches, but otherwise he has a natural gift for switching off that probably explains why his oft-delayed retirement is still a very distant day indeed.

Too many people have underrated Neil and bracketed him as a lower league manager because of his modest background. The fact is that he has done a good job wherever he has been in a career spanning a dozen clubs. He has literally worked his way up from the bottom and should be respected more for that. After a modest playing career as a journeyman winger in the lower reaches, Neil learned the ropes with Gainsborough, Burton and Scarborough, taking the latter into the Football League. He comes from the old school of bosses like Howard Wilkinson and Jim Smith who served a solid apprenticeship.

Throw in Warnock's experience with Notts County, Torquay, Huddersfield, Plymouth, Oldham, Bury, Sheffield United and Queens Park Rangers and you have the complete manager who is equipped to succeed at all levels. There is a certain charisma about the guy and you will hardly hear a bad word said about him by any player. That says a great deal for his man-management skills. So I'm really pleased for Neil that, at the time of writing, he was going great guns with QPR, a club who can finally free him of his shoestring background. Yes, he made some mistakes during his last tilt at the Premiership with the Blades but no-one is more deserving of another crack at it. And this time under wealthy owners who can help lift his career to a new peak.

Bryan Robson's appointment in Warnock's place proved to be an expensive mistake by Sheffield United. One argument was that he was judged too quickly by the club and another was that the fans never gave him an even break. There is some merit in the first and the second was undeniably true. The other side of the coin was that, with the players at his disposal plus costly acquisitions like James Beattie, United should have walked it to promotion.

Actually, the problem was that they tried to play their way there. Robson and the board wanted a change of culture; the former England captain imposed it too quickly and the players were caught in a conflict of styles. But I found Robson, whose man-management had been questioned at Middlesbrough, to be a likeable character. He wasn't blessed with great PR skills—which was a jolt following someone like Warnock—and it was near impossible to get him talking on the phone. But, face to face, he was friendly and accommodating and it was sad to see his reign end so quickly.

Hillsborough has been more the home of the revolving door during my time. The common denominator was a barely changing board of directors. One chairman who tried to break the mould was Dave Allen, the casino owner who gambled a lot of his own money as the only director in Hillsborough history to back the club in hard cash. At first, Allen was hostile to me because I speculated on potential takeovers even after he had joined the board in 2000.

One of those stories unveiled a sensational link with Sheffield's champion boxer Naseem Hamed—known variously as Prince

Naseem or just plain 'Naz' by his fans in the city. A source suggested Naz's family were in league with a Leeds businessman called Jeff Samuel in an effort to buy Wednesday. I tracked down Samuel who confirmed his designs on Hillsborough but volunteered nothing more than that. When I threw Hamed's name into the conversation, he was clearly uncomfortable, not wanting it to appear that he might have divulged a link which—from his reaction—clearly had some credence.

I struck a deal with Samuel that in the *Sheffield Telegraph* the following week I would write a story merely confirming his interest—and that I would only introduce the Naseem Hamed connection a week later. He was grateful and in an attempt to show it asked if I was a betting man. I said I wasn't. Undeterred, Samuel whispered the name of a horse running at Ascot the following Saturday and said it was a sure-fire winner. Out of curiosity more than anything, I placed a bet. But I was never to find out if I was wise to or not because the meeting was abandoned after a bomb scare just before the race in question!

The journalistic timetable went more according to plan. Before the following week's sensational *Sheffield Telegraph* story went to press—and also one I had sold to the *Daily Express*—I took the precaution of phoning Naz's brother Riath, who handled his business affairs, to run the Sheffield Wednesday link past him. He confirmed an interest on the record, which made it even better. Further, I was able to answer honestly and to allay his suspicions when he asked whether Jeff Samuel was my source. In absolute candour, I said he most definitely wasn't.

This story undoubtedly irritated Dave Allen. Actually, he was right to be upset because, as he must have suspected, it fizzled out to nothing. It annoyed me that Naz later laughed off the speculation as if it had been an invention, even though it had been substantiated by his brother.

But I didn't realise Allen intended to plough some of his fortune into Sheffield Wednesday and when he did, I wrote a comment piece saying that the fans should back him, even though I had no particular reason to support the bloke. A few days later, Dave broke his vow of silence and rang me to arrange a meeting. 'It's time we spoke face to face,' he said. I found him to be a fairly dogmatic character but straight talking and honest—and we have had a close rapport ever since.

We've had disagreements because I'm also not afraid to speak my mind—if not quite so bluntly as Dave!—and revealing this may surprise the anti-Allen faction who had me down as his stooge. I had a record of fall-outs with directors on both sides of the city, so I like to think I am nobody's mouthpiece. But I genuinely believed in Dave and the job he was doing, which is why I took his side. Yes, he could be rude and antagonistic, often dictatorial in his approach. But he made no apologies for any of this. Tough times require strong leaders.

If only he had been blessed with a modicum of diplomacy, I am convinced Allen would not have encountered the opposition that dissuaded him from investing more in the club. He would often tell me that his £3.5m stake was only for starters and that he had another £10m waiting if things settled down. This was no bluff—he has since ploughed £7.5m into Chesterfield. But for the antagonism that was partly self-inflicted, I am convinced Allen—who received little thanks for gifting Wednesday around £1m in fees and player wages—would ultimately have taken his place in history as the best, most resourceful Wednesday chairman of the modern era.

A classic example was when he came to a press conference armed with a withdrawal letter on behalf of would-be investor Paul Gregg, the former Everton director, which effectively said that he feared too much interference from the minority of fans who had hounded Allen. Dave read it out, which was all he needed to do to make his point. Instead, in launching into an astonishing outburst, he then branded some supporters 'scumbags' and 'cretins'. Not all but some. A minority of militants, if you like. Still, the damage was done. Allen's main point was overtaken by sensational stories about his attack on supporters and he became embroiled in an escalating row. There is no way even a staunch ally like myself could condone the language he used, even though you could understand the raw emotion behind it. This was after Allen had been told to 'Fuck off' in front of his own grandchildren by the sort of people who could most assuredly be described as 'scumbags' and 'cretins'.

Bit it was understandably offensive to supporters well beyond his intended targets and all hell let loose. People in public positions just can't afford to speak in those terms, whatever the provocation. I was glad to escape on holiday the very next day and I then gave the outburst issue a wide berth out of a sense of loyalty to a good contact. But actually it went beyond that. For all my sins and for all his faults, I liked and respected the bloke. He's loyal, too, by the way.

The fact is that DA's outspoken nature is part of the animal and you can't change that. His greatest strength—his no-nonsense candour—could be his weakness at times. Equally, his weakness—his lack of tact—could be a strength in running a tight ship threatened by mutiny. Allen's departure from Hillsborough was very regrettable and Wednesday's subsequent slide—they were comfortably placed in the Championship at the time—would appear to bear out the truth of this. In retrospect, I feel it was the silent majority of fans who let him down. They seemed broadly in support of him but washed their hands of all the politics.

What DA needed was a right-hand man like Wednesday's former secretary Graham Mackrell, a smooth operator who can sweeten any pill while maintaining control. It needed to be good cop-bad cop. Allen seemed to grasp this at one point and I sounded out Graham on his behalf. Nothing happened from there, unfortunately. I heard a rumour later that the rest of the board had vetoed the plan to bring him back. If so, more fool them, in my opinion.

Without a skilled inside operator like Mackrell to act as a bridge with the manager, the job became even more difficult for men like

Chris Turner, who built what turned into a promotion side and who was unfortunate to be sacked early one season. But what really accounted for Turner was the Ken Bates ownership bid engulfing the club in September 2004. It had rumbled for months when Turner departed to be replaced by a proven promotion-winner in Paul Sturrock.

Naturally, I took Allen's side in helping him to rebuff Bates. The ex-Chelsea chief eventually withdrew in the face of mounting opposition, and also the appointment of Sturrock, which even Bates knew to be a smart move.

I took a hit from a fiery episode that became highly personal on all sides. Soon afterwards, by which time Bates had moved to Leeds, I was refused entry to a game at Elland Road for Final Score in March, 2006. When I queried this, Bates referred me to my press cuttings, which he said unnecessarily denigrated him. He concluded his letter: 'You are not welcome here.' I took this on the chin, while pointing out that all I had done was to be loyal to the chairman I was working with and with whom I got on well. As I would perhaps have done for Bates himself in other circumstances, you never know. The gap between enmity and friendship can be incredibly close, as evidenced by my experience with Allen.

What I can't understand is why the ban—at the time of writing— is still in place years later. I pride myself on being too professional to let such an issue cloud my judgment of Leeds as a team or the club as a whole. Indeed, I haven't referred publicly to the previous clash other than the obvious need to do so here. And I believe the chairman of Leeds, an indomitable character who displays a ferocious determination to succeed, should take due credit for reviving a once-great club. However, considering that most of the articles that offended Bates were in the local rather than national press, I am surprised that a big-hitter like him should find a small-timer like me important enough to bar—for life, it would seem.

By the way, I heard about Paul Sturrock's appointment by Wednesday in advance and broke the story in the *Daily Mail*. Chris

Kamara rang that morning, presumably to see if it was worth getting a bet on! Hope he did. I didn't, even though I knew it to be true. I've never been into gambling but broke my resolve a few years later, as you'll hear. Sturrock was a good manager and an affable, homespun character who was helpful to me despite my allegiance to his boss. He would often refer to the *Sheffield Telegraph* as the 'chairman's bugle'. But he did it to my face, which I respected. There were times when I was trapped between two men who were clearly at odds and was careful not to disclose a confidence either way. But all was not well and a supposed new deal handed to Sturrock after a bout of infighting was not at all what it seemed.

Just as I knew about Paul's arrival, I had a fair idea about his departure, much as it stunned the club's fans. The grapevine told me in advance of a home game with Barnsley that, if Wednesday didn't win, Sturrock would be out that night. Sure enough, they were shambling towards a disappointing 1–1 draw and, ominously, chairman Allen stood up to leave the directors box with a few minutes to go. From the boardroom, he will have heard the cheers as Chris Brunt scored a brilliant last-minute winner. I announced on *Final Score* that this had kept Sturrock in a job. But he was to last only another few days, departing after a heavy midweek defeat at Colchester. I was proved right but still sorry because Paul was an honourable man. Nevertheless, Allen had made a brave decision fearlessly and did not deserve the furious public backlash he then suffered. Further, the results improved immeasurably under first caretaker Sean McAuley and then a new boss in Brian Laws, lured from Scunthorpe.

Laws lasted over three years—even outreaching Allen's reign as chairman—to become the longest-serving Wednesday boss since Trevor Francis. As a communicator, he was one of the best I've worked with and handled himself classily at all times. Every time he was on the ropes—which was three times in all before the axe fell—he took questions about his future on the chin. Eventually, like so many before him, he lost the unequal battle with the club's finances after a series of questionable signings.

I feared Laws faced a prolonged spell in the wilderness but just a few weeks later, his name surfaced among favourites for the job at former club Burnley, then trying to hold on to their place in the Premiership. It seemed a highly improbable development but I made some enquiries and a good contact told me Laws had as good as got the job. I sold this to the *Daily Mail* as an exclusive—and then got greedy. Maybe it was time I did have a bet.

Brian was only evens in the bookies odds but there was still a killing to be made if I had the courage of my convictions. So I placed bets totalling £350 on Laws to get the Burnley job. This was much to the annoyance of my wife Lynne, although I took the precaution of not telling her the exact figure! Suddenly the odds started changing, but not in the way I'd hoped. Doncaster's Sean O'Driscoll overtook Laws and was rapidly installed as the 4–1-on favourite. Surely the bookies couldn't be that wrong and I resigned myself to losing a chunk of cash and having a big bite taken out of my credibility with the *Mail*.

But my 48 hour emotional ringer took yet another twist when Laws went back to Burnley for another 'interview' when he was actually confirmed in the job. I heard later that Burnley had ruled out O'Driscoll a few days earlier but had played out the drama to make it look as if they were considering all their options. Whatever, I was delighted but mostly relieved. I have resolved never to chance my arm in that way again.

15

THE OTHER SIDE OF THE FENCE

I had long wondered how managers and players coped with personal abuse—until I experienced it myself. The manifestation occurred during Dave Allen's controversial chairmanship of Sheffield Wednesday and continued even after he left as a small but vociferous group of anonymous supporters targeted me unmercifully on a fans' website. Comments ranged from the comical ('Biggs deserves to have his testicles clamped in a rusty bulldog clip') to the insulting ('he's an effing idiot'). There were calls for me to be sacked by the *Sheffield Telegraph* and libellous claims that I was incapable of doing my job.

At first it was too much of a novelty to be upsetting. I even chuckled at my sudden notoriety, laughed along with some of the wittier put-downs and struggled to believe that people were taking it all so seriously. For journalists to be pilloried in public is something of a new phenomenon. I am not alone here. Several others on the South Yorkshire scene have suffered . . . people like Paul Walker, Seth Bennett and Andy Giddins of BBC Radio Sheffield, Ian Appleyard of the *Yorkshire Post* and, to a lesser extent, Paul Thompson and James Shield of the *Sheffield Star*. Even so, I appeared to have no rival as Public Enemy Number One for a section of Sheffield Wednesday fans.

It's interesting because it provides an insight into what players and managers routinely experience, albeit on a much larger scale. The main and most obvious difference is that we are not actually shouted at. That said, I found myself laughing again as I formed the mental picture of a hack bending over his computer keyboard, trying to compose an article while encircled by an angry mob of people all yelling in his ear.

Then again, not one of the keyboard warriors who have abused me has appeared from behind his pseudonym to speak to me personally, maybe to approach me at a game or in the street. I'd have more respect for them if they did. One at a time, though, please! I'd be happy enough to argue the toss, providing it was civilised and respectful on both sides. There's nothing wrong with a difference of opinion. Fans are fully entitled to their views about journalists, just as with players and managers.

I've ridden with a lot of it, actually finding it a valuable experience. For instance, I've sampled a little of the frustration felt by performers who can't answer back. As former Wednesday captain Lee Bullen said to me recently: 'Welcome to our world.' Bullen, still a keen follower of the club, had seen a lot of the postings. 'It's the first time I've known a journalist get such treatment,' he added.

We shared a laugh about it, but there are still times when forum contributors cross the line and when website managers should be more vigilant about what they allow. The limits on what is acceptable seem to be too blurred. I admit there was a period when it got under my skin and I forced an apology to be posted. Now I don't take it quite so seriously—or so personally as I realise that I was used as a surrogate punchbag for former chairman Allen. Not that I regret the relationship with him, despite being caught in the crossfire.

Also, I have taken to following my own advice—that is, the recommendation I have always given managers on the many occasions when they have confided their anger and upset about what is said about them on phone-ins or websites. 'Don't listen, don't look—just ignore it and they can't get to you,' is what I've always urged. That, of course, is easier said than done, as I've now discovered. But it does work. I don't take any notice anymore unless I'm put in the position where I have to. Only a little filters through—the stuff you are told about—and that's the right balance. It's as well to have people keeping an eye out just in case it crosses the line.

Those who really know me would tell you, I hope, that I'm a pretty reasonable sort of chap, certainly non-aggressive and not consumed by hate. And I'm experienced enough to know that when things are not going right at a football club, people will lash out in all directions.

Sheffield Wednesday fans have suffered more than most down the years. What poisoned the atmosphere is that for too long the club had ineffectual leadership from the top—and therefore it had too many voices around it. By and large, journalists write things based on what they are told. There are bad apples in any trade, but the vast majority of us don't just invent stuff, contrary to some beliefs!

But there comes a point in a takeover saga when you just don't know who to believe anymore. And the casualties of misinformation, the build-up of hopes and all the false trails, are the fans who hang on every word about their club. Small wonder, I suppose, that they start to become cynical about everything they read. You are giving them the dream and then dashing it over and over again. Not on purpose, I should add. We can't be responsible for possibilities not coming to fruition. But you have to weigh up the frustration of fans and understand it. More than that, I can assure them I shared it! Thank goodness for Milan Mandaric buying the club late in 2010 and putting us all out of our misery. All, that is, including Howard Wilkinson who had stepped into the breach as an emergency chairman and who was glad to pass on such an improbable and burdensome role, mightily relieved that his beloved club had been saved from administration. Take a bow,

Howard.

Once upon a time, supporters had too little say on the running of their clubs. There was the odd letters page and an occasional phone -in. Do they now have too much say? Certainly, the drip, drip, drip of public opinion, some of it misguided and uninformed, can have a dangerous effect. Falsehoods can become projected as truths by the sheer weight of numbers expressing an opinion. If enough people say that Joe Bloggs is a bad manager long enough and loudly enough then, as sure as United follows Manchester, Joe Bloggs will be removed from office. I feel the media has to look for some kind of balance on public forums in football, despite their obvious popularity and the fact that it amounts to cheap broadcasting.

Maybe it's all arisen because clubs have shifted away from their dependence on fans as customers who were the lifeblood of their existence. Television income and marketing deals have taken over, particularly at the top level where the paying fan is almost incidental and that can't be healthy. Is it any wonder that fans are fighting back? It would be far healthier if they were still the main revenue stream, only treated accordingly rather than ignored as they were in the past. Wake me up, I'm dreaming!

Talking of which, I used to pinch myself in the old days at Hallam when I would have people asking for signed photographs. More recently, I've been on a metaphorical wanted poster. Having seen such extremes of public reaction, I can attest to the truth of the old saying that you should never believe your own publicity.

16

WHERE ARE THEY NOW?

Answer: nowhere. Otherwise known as League One. Hence this book is partly a bid to make good lost earnings! Aside from one false dawn at Bramall Lane, England's fifth largest city has been absent from the Premier League for a whole decade. It started with Paul Jewell exiting stage left at Hillsborough in 2001 within a few months of delivering some powerful opening lines. This was a blood-curdling battle cry that could have come straight from a Shakespeare play. When I parked myself in Jewell's office that August day, I hadn't bargained for his scathing attack on the overpaid, under-achieving players he had inherited from the club's relegation.

He basically told them to shape up or ship out. Of course, they couldn't be shifted under the weight of their fat contracts and the only rearrangement of furniture saw the rug swiftly tugged from under the manager's feet. Dave Allen was a bystander to this decision, having only just joined the board but he later recognised the club's mistake as Jewell went on to top his previous promotion and survival act with Bradford. This time he lifted Wigan Athletic two divisions and only left—on his own terms—after they had won at Bramall Lane to dump the Blades on a dramatic last day in 2007.

The reverberations from that result are still being felt by the Blades. Even without hindsight, Neil Warnock was probably the best man to bring them back. After he left and United suffered again from the ill-judged appointment of Bryan Robson, Kevin

Blackwell rekindled the club. But Blackwell then succumbed at the beginning of his third full season, which can often be pivotal, while across the city Alan Irvine was the man charged with reversing a continuation of a Sheffield Wednesday decline that was largely beyond his control—before being replaced by Gary Megson. It's astonishing that, aside from Leeds' promotion, Rotherham were the most successful club in Yorkshire in the 2009–10 season—for getting to a play-off final they lost.

It was good to see Ronnie Moore back in charge of the Millers; a real extrovert character who is never short of a word. There were two promotions last time, plus good work in between for Tranmere. Rock on, Ronnie. During his previous spell at Rotherham, Moore was at the centre of a quite extraordinary episode.

On the eve of a home game in October, 2002, a story broke of an official approach for his services from Ipswich Town. Rotherham then confirmed this, having apparently been called by Town chairman David Sheepshanks, and Ronnie went on to entertain the interest. He as good as said he would take the job during a range of post-match interviews. Having waited so long for such an opportunity, no-one at Millmoor begrudged his excitement about leaving.

Then it emerged that 'Ipswich's call' to Millmoor was a hoax. This was verified by the Suffolk club who were left baffled by weekend headlines that Moore was about to become their new manager. Embarrassment all round.

The sequel to this story is not so well known. After the weekend, Ipswich *did* make an official approach to Rotherham, as I discovered at the time. They were alerted by the hoax story itself, realising that it might be a good idea to play out the drama for real. Moore was a successful manager who deserved a bigger opportunity and, from his quotes, he obviously wanted the job.

So, under the smokescreen of the farce, Rotherham came to field a genuine enquiry. Whether they realised it or not is another matter. By this time they didn't know what was real and what wasn't. Not wanting to risk further ridicule, Rotherham refused Ipswich's actual request and hushed it up. You had to feel sorry for Ronnie all over again as he was left in limbo with a club struggling to hold on to second tier status. I put out the story of the real approach but by then everyone was so confused that it barely saw the light of day.

At Sheffield United, Blackwell played out his own drama after the club's play-off final defeat to Burnley in 2009. He offered to quit at a time when Queens Park Rangers were courting him. Then Blackwell pulled back after being persuaded to stay by chairman McCabe and QPR's efforts were rebuffed by the board. However, Blackwell's fears about United's immediate future were realised. Cash cutbacks combined with an injury crisis to create an unstoppable loss of momentum. Despite this, the Blades still finished comfortably in the top half in 2010 and only a few points adrift of the play-offs. This didn't match the club's ambitions, of course, or appease the fans, but Blackwell regarded it as his finest work as a manager and I have to say that, in all the circumstances, I agree with him.

The trouble was that frustration clouded an objective view and at times Kevin struggled to contain his own, even though he understood that the club's priority had switched to responsible housekeeping amid a worldwide recession that profoundly threatened the football industry. He knew, as well, that the opening weeks or months of the 2010–11 campaign would be critical for him.

What he couldn't have imagined — in fact, nobody did — was that he would be sacked after just two league games, the first a commendable draw at Cardiff. There followed a defeat at Hartlepool in the Carling Cup with a pretty strong line-up, albeit with a weak bench that underlined Blackwell's problems. Then came a 3–0 home defeat to Neil Warnock's Queens Park Rangers. Blackwell was sacked immediately afterwards.

I was at Blackburn that day, reporting for *Final Score*. When I climbed into my car at 5.45 and started hearing the first radio rumours of Kevin's demise, it was one of those times when you have to grip the wheel to stay on the road. As someone charged with being on top of events at Bramall Lane, you doubt yourself in circumstances like these. You are not supposed to be shocked. Then again, this was a nasty surprise for the victim himself. Blackwell knew, and accepted, that he would probably be judged after seven or eight games; he had no idea he would last only two.

Yet I am reliably informed that the events of that day also came as something of a surprise to the man who wielded the axe, chairman Kevin McCabe. It was not, we were told, a case of him driving to the ground in the expectation of acting if United lost. But some defeats seem worse than others. Warnock was back in town, for starters, and so was goalkeeper Paddy Kenny, promised a rough ride in goal for Rangers after defecting from Bramall Lane where the Blades had stood by him in the face of a lengthy drugs ban the previous season. Kenny was a spectator as United slipped to a defeat that was hard for their fans to stomach. And McCabe, too.

Whether it was a board decision is unclear, bearing in mind that Blackwell was summoned immediately after the game. Subsequently I heard rumours that other directors were as surprised by the decision as anyone else. Then again, McCabe, as majority shareholder and a huge benefactor to the club, was entitled to act as he saw fit. But it was an uncharacteristic deed by a chairman who had always prided himself on avoiding kneejerk reactions. Certainly, it became hard to refute the argument that, if Blackwell was on such rocky ground, the change would have been better made at the end of the previous season.

Whatever else, though, McCabe is an honourable man whose reputation for treating his managers fairly is well earned. He settled Blackwell's compensation claim with similar alacrity, reaching an agreement within a month of the change. And it's satisfying to report that the pair have remained on friendly terms. The bottom line in football these days is that finance governs everything. Sheffield United are one of those clubs where the lack of Premiership football is biting deepest.

There's no mystery or shame about any of this because all clubs, outside an elite few, are having to economise as the excesses of the past come back to haunt them in a harsh financial climate. Bear in mind that the Blades are renowned as a well-run outfit, so the extent of the problem is huge. It's just a pity that the consequences of obscene player wages have yet to fully hit the clubs who created this unsustainable spiral. Yes, Manchester United and Liverpool are quaking a little. But Manchester City are showing that mega-rich foreign owners aren't yet ready to abandon football as their sexy new toy.

All the rest can do is ensure they don't get sucked into the vortex by chasing the dream. But so many are suffering that a warning is hardly necessary. And fans at all levels are having to accept that success at any price is not worth having. So it's hard not to conclude that men like Blackwell, with an excellent record from his time at Leeds, have to be trusted for doing the best possible job in difficult circumstances — rather than thrown overboard whenever fans want a change. Irvine, too, looked a more than safe pair of hands for Sheffield Wednesday. His sacking by Preston, following two successful years, was ridiculously harsh. Although the Owls were relegated under his command, he had put the Owls back on course when Milan Mandaric's takeover proved his undoing after some well-intentioned help in the transfer market backfired.

Happily for the likes of me, all Sheffield's recent bosses have been good to deal with in their different ways. All managers have their own methods with the media — when they are allowed to employ them. At too many clubs, their appearances are stage-managed by press officers and there is little opportunity for journalists to talk to them outside these times. Crucially, personal relationships still count for something in Sheffield. Maybe there is an irony here in that the lesser profile of the Championship and League One has made the job easier in that sense. But you would like to think that personal access would remain in place even in the Premier League — as a working model for those clubs who stifle it.

I'm thankful that I can still call the managers I work with and hope this never changes. When it does, it will be the time I quit newspaper reporting during the week and concentrate purely on match coverage.

You might not catch them first time—nor would you always expect to given the demands of their job—but Blackwell and Irvine are two managers who will either take calls or ring you back. Subsequently Gary Speed and Micky Adams too. And you can't ask for more than that. There are differences in that Kevin would often make time for a quick conversation while on the hoof, for instance driving between Bramall Lane and the training ground. Alan prefers to keep his daytimes clear so that he can immerse himself exclusively in the job. But he will clock your call and get back to you, sometimes when you least expect it. You can't put a value on this sort of co-operation and, looking through my career, I think I've been lucky with the help I've received from so many managers.

For me, it's never much of an issue when a manager or player dodges a particular question or refuses to talk altogether. It's normal and no offence should be taken. The media has become such a pervading presence that you can't blame public figures for running for cover occasionally and, besides, we have no entitlement to co-operation. But I make an exception for rudeness.

Former Republic of Ireland manager Steve Staunton completely blanked my reasonable attempts to talk to him after a game he had played for Aston Villa in the early 1990s. He just walked past as if I was invisible when a simple 'No, I'd rather not' or a 'Not now, I've got to get away' would have sufficed. These days the lack of courtesy is less overt . . . players simply walk past with their mobiles glued to their ears.

Another player who I have experienced failing to show any manners was Paul Ince. It was after a game at Anfield in 1998 between Ince's Liverpool and newly-crowned champions Arsenal. I was on interviewing duty for 5 Live and positioned in the dressing room corridor with the full permission of the home club. As the former Manchester United and England midfielder neared me, I uttered a polite: 'Excuse me, Paul.' He looked the other way and carried on walking, albeit in no particular hurry. In fact, he was ambling to such an extent that I had time to utter 'Paul?' twice more from a range of no more than two feet. It was as if he had gone stone deaf as he made no eye contact and seemed to pretend I didn't exist.

He didn't want to be interviewed apparently! No big deal. Why not have the decency to say so then? That type of incident could only perpetuate a reputation for arrogance surrounding Ince, once the self-styled 'Governor' of the Old Trafford dressing room. I can't say whether or not it is deserved because I simply don't know the man. In the same place on the same night a young England striker called Michael Owen duly obliged and spoke with great maturity. Impressions are indelibly formed by exchanges of this sort.

I wouldn't mind so much were it not for the fact that in later years Ince has used the media to ply a new trade as a newspaper columnist. And he's not the only difficult interviewee to have courted the media when it suits them. At least there is nothing two-faced about Sir Alex Ferguson in this regard. He routinely gives a good kicking to people in our trade and never attempts to put the boot on the other foot by cashing in as a pundit.

However, it's equally fair to point out that Fergie will probably be the last of his type. His wonderful football methodology may have stood the test of time but he is a dinosaur in PR terms. Surely no other manager will enjoy his sort of power and latitude to be a law unto himself with the press, radio and television. It simply won't be tolerated. Like it or not, the modern manager has to accept that media relations are part of his job. He may still have the occasional personal issue with a particular reporter or organisation, but a prolonged refusal to talk to a powerful national outlet like the BBC will, I feel, never be seen again.

Football and the media have to remember three things amid this asphyxiating age of in-house spin doctoring. First, it's a two-way street. There has to be give and take for a successful relationship. Second—and this is mainly aimed at the clubs—there is no such thing as proper praise without fair criticism. Website platitudes to players and managers are utterly worthless unless they are pitched against an objective background. Fans are too knowledgeable to be fooled by some of the tripe trotted out by the clubs in the misguided belief that they are providing a news service for supporters. Thirdly, and most importantly, the game and the media cannot live without each other. Let's get on with it.

17

SOME PEOPLE ARE ON THE PITCH ... BUT IT'S NOT ALL OVER YET!

I wound up the 2009–10 season back at my spiritual home of Saltergate—for the last time. There were people on the pitch at the end, hundreds of them, as I delivered what I proudly believe to be the last national broadcast from the ground where Chesterfield had played for well over a century. This was on *Final Score*, though I also doubled up for 5 Live that day.

At one point, the game was so poor that the occasion was in danger of going flat. But old mate, John Smith, (the Matlock fan who helped launch my career at Wembley) came to the rescue yet again. First, I should explain that it can be impossible to take sustenance or even go for a wee at half-time because of the timing of reports. So it was that afternoon, though there really wasn't much to say as the game drifted into the second half. Then John kindly presented me with a sandwich plucked from the press room at the break. The very last one. Listeners around the country and all over the globe on the BBC's World Service heard tell of my eating a 'ceremonial sandwich . . . the last ever to be served up at Saltergate'. As it happened, there was to be a tasty end to the game itself as Derek Niven fittingly won it for Chesterfield with a cracker of a goal in stoppage time.

But you are always thankful for these sort of diversions. Colleague Peter Cooper created a hilarious sideshow for his fellow scribes at Sheffield Wednesday matches in the 1980s. The Owls had a very reputable striker called Imre Varadi, in fact a prolific scorer for clubs including Newcastle United. But Imre couldn't always hit the target and some of his attempts would be quite wayward. Coops organised a sweep involving the names on all the advertising placards behind each goal and there would be a pre-match draw. Whenever a Varadi shot hit one of those boards, the 'owner' would hit the jackpot—as I did once with the princely sum of about £20.

Let me add that Imre got to hear about this and took it in good part. The truth is—and no bullshit here—that we couldn't have had such fun at the expense of just any player. It had to be one who was guaranteed to get in shots at goal. If you don't shoot, you don't score . . . that's a time-honoured motto. Varadi is a good example of a player who, to quote another very true cliché, is never afraid to miss. Bless him!

I digress. Back to Chesterfield who, at the time of writing, are going great guns under the management of John Sheridan. After their move on to pastures new, with Dave Allen as boardroom benefactor, I look forward to many more years in press boxes around the country. Football reporting is hardly a job where you aspire to retirement. Don't tell anyone, will you, but I'd almost be tempted to do it for nothing. Which is perhaps just as well with all the belt-tightening taking place in our industry, particularly newspapers! I know there are people out there who'd gladly pay to do a job like mine. How long before they are taken up on it?

Certainly, there has been a major downturn in the story market for freelances. A number of factors have put the squeeze on me, mostly outside my control. First there is the grim reality that papers rarely look outside the Premiership for material these days. They don't editionise any more for a start and there is a polarisation towards the top four or five clubs, plus a day-in day-out obsession with the Beckhams and the Rooneys. Secondly, my area has been in decline for far too long. No Premiership means less income. And third, papers would much rather fill their pages in house than pay an outside agency.

In fairness, I should add that as your contacts get older the sources can dry up. But even coming up with stories isn't a guarantee that there is a target area to hit because of the media's overriding obsession with the big stuff. One day some enlightened editor will wake up to the idea that there is an awful loss of interest in the Championship, a hugely competitive league boasting any number of clubs who are better supported than several of those in the Premier League. In the meantime, it's good to see my old *Express* sports editor David Emery making a go of it with the *Football League Paper*.

Another problem for the likes of me is the rolling 24-hour format of the modern news media. The proliferation of websites, blogs and Twitter accounts means that information is immediate. Just think of the time lapse between filing a story and it appearing in a newspaper the next day. It can become old news within a matter of minutes let alone hours. So papers tend to drive their own agendas and give news a themed type treatment.

A desire to simply stand still is not one of life's magic formulas—but it can be an achievement in itself in this highly competitive business. That's why I admire people like my *Final Score* reporting colleague, Harry Gration, the veteran television anchor for BBC *Look North*. Harry, a natural presenter, makes it all look so effortless. Which, of course, it isn't. Then there are those of my generation like Damian Johnson, another BBC football reporter, and David Hirst, of Yorkshire Television news and sport, whose professionalism continues to hold back the hordes of wannabees.

So I take pride in longevity more than anything else. On any Saturday afternoon in winter there will be around 90 commentators and reporters broadcasting nationally on football. There are millions, literally, who would want to take our places. Same with the newspaper journalists. Staying there is harder than getting there, believe me. But a lot of it is down to luck and none of us should ever lose sight of our great fortune . . . even if I have to confess the downturn in the newspaper market has left me a lot less busy these days.

All of which has left me with an excess of creative energy that I have tried to channel into this book. The need to turn a negative into a positive can be a powerful stimulus. So I've enacted an idea I have toyed with for some time—but this still reaches you 10 years earlier than intended! Another plus from a minus is that I've had the time to become a regular half-marathon runner, a peculiar and painful hobby that few of the many who do it can properly explain. I mention this purely by way of an unashamed plug for a running appeal on behalf of Sheffield Children's Hospital! Donations can be made by logging onto www.justgiving.com/alan-biggs. Cheeky or what?

18

REFS TO THE RESCUE

The main reason I have lasted for over 25 years as a journalist on the national scene is that, with Keith Hackett's help, I found a niche as a specialist on refereeing stories. There was a time when this was uncharted territory and I claimed it as my own as referees became more high-profile and therefore big news. It's a sad fact of life that they only tend to be newsworthy in controversial circumstances, usually because they have made a mistake. And, as I often tell them, I make more money when they do! So I'm always at risk of being called two-faced in my support for them.

However, I have tried to balance the criticism with many a story about the development of referees into a highly professional unit that Hackett, on becoming manager of Professional Game Match Officials, memorably called 'the 21st team in the Premiership'. Keith's insight, and the spread of contacts I have made through him, has given me a rare understanding of referees and what makes them tick. They are badly misunderstood. Most of them are nice guys, unfailingly honest and only in it for the love of the game. They are said to crave being the centre of attention but, in all but a few cases, I believe this to be a fundamental myth. On a private basis, I have occasionally shared the anguish of referees—Howard Webb for instance—after they have made a high profile mistake. They don't relish that sort of exposure, believe me.

It was clear from an off-the-record chat with Webb, during an open day at the referees' training base in Warwick, that he was his own biggest critic. The previous night—on 10th February 2010— Howard had taken charge of a game at the Emirates Stadium in which Arsenal beat Liverpool 1–0. Webb was still agonising over a late controversy that led to criticism from Liverpool manager Rafa Benitez. Replays of a Steven Gerrard free-kick showed Cesc Fabregas, who was in the Arsenal wall, escape punishment for a clear handling offence on the edge of the area.

Revealing Howard's private reaction is not a case of talking out of school, rather by way of demonstrating his conscientious nature and the attention to detail that has taken him to the very top. The modern referee does listen to complaints and is intent on learning from any mistake, even though human errors can never be fully eradicated. Howard accepted that Benitez was right in that he had missed the offence, although whether it should have been a free kick or a penalty was debatable. Where Howard was most self-critical was over his positioning. He admitted he'd put himself at the wrong angle. Of course, his soul-searching was not made public at the time and most apologies to managers—normally accepted more graciously than people might imagine—are usually made in private. But I mention the incident to highlight the fact that referees take the job very seriously and don't brush away their mistakes.

Little could I have realised, and certainly not Howard, that at the end of the campaign he would take charge of both the Champions League Final and the World Cup final in a couple of magical, monumental months. Thus Howard became the first referee to bring up that Utopian double.

But I should not have been surprised. Keith Hackett had made me a bold, public prediction that his long-time protégé would not only succeed at the World Cup but would also be handed the final—providing England weren't in it, of course. No worries on that score! I know Keith pretty well. He's normally circumspect and, if anything, understated. It was telling of his trust in Howard's ability and temperament that Keith had no worries about putting his man under pressure with local and national headlines tipping him for the final. He knew he could handle it. And he did, whatever Holland might say.

I exchanged texts with Howard—who I'd known since before his introduction to the Premier League—throughout the tournament in South Africa. He is always courteous about answering messages, and considering the number he must have received, I was struck by the reply he took the trouble to send after his selection for the final. It read: 'Thanks so much for your message mate. I really appreciate it. Been an amazing few hours, feel so honoured and privileged. I'm lucky that I've got great lads in my team. Speak soon mate. H.'

Of course, that promise became impossible to keep because he was absolutely inundated and desperately needed a rest. There are times as a journalist when you have to back off and not crowd people, whatever the demands of the job. Webb was confronted with a beast of a game courtesy of disgraceful tactics from the Dutch who put their own reputation for 'total football' to the sword. No referee could have handled the game better given the almost impossible circumstances. Howard will have taken no pleasure, only sadness from handing out 14 yellow cards and one red—a record for a final. But he had no option and emerged with the credit he deserved for keeping control as the English media rallied round.

Just watching the game was an ordeal for anyone who knew Howard, so I can't imagine what his family went through. I found it hard enough myself. And difficult afterwards to consciously keep my distance and not intrude—against all my journalistic instincts. I just felt so close to it and yet so far from it. Best, I felt, to back off unless Keith specifically wanted to involve me, not least because any attempt I made to back Howard would have carried less weight because of the vested interest. And best for Keith, along with the Premier League, to speak to the media as a whole. Every man and his dog wanted a piece of the action. That and the fact that Howard was being well supported were further reasons for letting the stampede go over my head. You strive to make good contacts, but there are times when you can be too close to a subject. My various outlets seemed to understand this and the phone stayed surprisingly quiet until later that week.

Nonetheless, Howard texted back a few days after his return: 'Hi Alan. Still adjusting back to normality. The World Cup was an amazing experience for us and to get to the final was such an honour. Although it was a tough match we feel very proud of how we performed in South Africa. I just want to say a huge thanks for all your support pal. I appreciate it so much. H.'

That's the kind of guy we're talking about here and there are many more like him. Our top footballers all too often send the wrong moral message to kids but there is no doubt that referees like Howard are perfect role models. Through his example, there's more chance than ever of reversing the culture of ridicule and hatred towards match officials and accepting them as a very necessary part of the game. Webb's performance in South Africa must have done wonders for the FA's Respect initiative and for the recruitment of young officials, which unsurprisingly had been a major problem. Also I detect a change in the media's attitude towards referees and that's important too.

What has hurt many referees more than anything over the years is the feeling that they are not trusted by the powers that be to make sensible public comment. And yet these are mature guys in their thirties, forties and even fifties. Hence most of my conversations with referees have been off the record. They have become punchbags, absorbing unwarranted attacks from managers and players without any right of reply. Like many of the officials themselves, I have always believed that a lot of this would stop if refs were routinely expected to clear up any issues with the media after a game. Quite often they are in the right but appear to be in the wrong if they can't explain a technical point or remove a misunderstanding. And if they are wrong, what's wrong with them saying so? That then takes the sting out of any criticism because all of us in life have greater respect for people who can hold their hands up and admit to a mistake; we all make them.

In these circumstances, I was pleased when Sir Alex Ferguson got his comeuppance after a wholly unjustified attack on Alan Wiley in October, 2009. And even more delighted to have played a part in defence of Wiley. Now don't get me wrong here, Sir Alex is a great manager and—unlike a few of my more exalted colleagues—there is no history between us. I have spoken to him a few times after games and although the issues have been less than combustible, he has always been civil. But his repeated hounding of referees, so often pushed under the carpet by a toothless FA, was beyond the pale.

So when Ferguson falsely claimed Wiley to be 'unfit' a line simply had to be drawn. At first, I thought Fergie would again escape scot free. It was more by way of going through the motions than the genuine hope of a follow-up story that I rang Wiley. It was not a cold call because we had spoken in the past (including a conversation about netball because his daughter played the game and he had heard me commentating on Sky . . . he also said the rules baffled him!) Alan has a wry sense of humour. He answered the phone by saying: 'I shouldn't be sat here talking to you. I should be out training because obviously I'm not fit!' I laughed but he was making a serious point and underneath it all was plainly very upset. But, of course, he had been told not to say anything.

Next day a moment of pure telepathy occurred. I knew that ProZone provided a detailed breakdown of referees' performances in every match and started wondering how I might access Wiley's details for the game in question. That, I felt, would be sure to nail Fergie's claim. This data was widely distributed to people across the higher echelons of football. Lo and behold, I then had a call from a well-placed contact in the game and after a few other enquiries I ended up with Wiley's very revealing statistics!

These sensationally showed, among other things, that he had actually run further than most of Ferguson's players. Naturally, I had a field day and so did the *Daily Mail*. Largely as a result,

Ferguson was forced to apologise—though his first attempt further inflamed referees because it repeated his view that foreign officials were fitter—and he eventually received a two-match touchline ban. In practice, this was nothing more than a rap across the knuckles. But it was the first time any manager had been banned for comments in the media, so a point had been forcibly made.

What I like about Fergie, though, is that, as ever, he took his punishment like a man. I think he also had a sneaking respect for the refs on this occasion in that for once they had shown the courage to stand up to him and hit back. And a particular admiration, maybe, for the fact that they had involved their union to defend Wiley. The irony of this cannot have gone unnoticed by this product of the Govan shipyards in Glasgow. Underneath it all, you suspect that even Sir Alex—no great fan of the FA—might feel the authorities have been too soft with him. No man stands for the value of good discipline more than him.

Unsurprisingly, sit-down interviews with referees are rare, at least while they are actively in the game. And even when they leave the middle it's usually to stay involved. As such, they remain entwined in red tape. I have lost count of the number of times I have approached ex-refs for a comment only to be told they daren't say anything because they were still in the organisation as an assessor or coach. So any kind of comment on a major flashpoint would often be impossible.

But there have been times when I have had the necessary approval to interview referees at length. Often, this would be before a showpiece like an FA Cup final. Graham Barber and Steve Lodge both gave me memorable pieces on that basis, as did Steve Bennett. The funny thing with Steve was that the last time I had come across him was when he was a baby! As a young child, I remember being taken by my parents to the home of their friends Eve and Eddie Bennett in the Kent countryside. On one visit, they had a new addition to the family.

Several decades later my dad pointed to the television during a game Steve was refereeing and said 'you remember Eve and Eddie, don't you . . . that's their son.' I heard that the Bennetts made a similar observation to Steve having heard me on the radio. Of course, he was too young to remember me from those far off days but we marvel at the coincidence and keep in touch.

Another interview that stands out was with Mark Halsey after he had completed a courageous recovery from cancer to resume his refereeing career in 2010. I was delighted to have the first in-depth chat with Mark for articles that appeared in the *News of the World* and the *Daily Mirror*. 'I feel like the guy who won £56m on the lottery,' he told me. 'One other thing the cancer has done for me— I've lost weight. And for another, my hair is growing back and my wife fancies me again!'

Amy Fearn, one of the female officials blazing a trail in the professional game, was quick to see the funny side when I interviewed her early in her career. She'd just run the line in a match I covered at Hillsborough where a witty colleague was quick to seize on a couple of controversial incidents involving the lady assistant referee. His *Sun* intro referred to 'Amy's two boobs'. She told me she'd seen the article and had laughed along, not the least offended. I guess you need a thick skin to be a woman in a man's world. All joking apart, there is absolutely no reason why women like Amy, following the earlier breakthrough of Wendy Toms, should not be standard bearers for many more female officials. This, by the way, was easily identifiable as banter—unlike the Sian Massey put-downs that subsequently cost Sky duo Richard Keys and Andy Gray their jobs. But it wouldn't be considered acceptable in the new climate and guess we all have to be more careful. If all of us were judged by our private remarks there would be nobody left working!

Whatever people say about them, refs are usually more than willing to share a laugh at their own expense—which is probably just as well. Hopefully they'll enjoy this. When my eldest daughter, Rosanna, was about six she joined my son and myself at her first proper game. You can't shield kids from the usual language, of course, and at one stage, there was a familiar burst of 'the referee's a wanker'. Rosanna must have taken note of this without hearing it quite right (fortunately). On the way home in the car, she suddenly burst into a chorus of 'the referee's a wagon, the referee's a wagon'. Father and brother were both in hysterics. Naturally, we couldn't bring ourselves to explain why!

Incidentally, it's amazing how much wisdom we all have after the event where refereeing mistakes are concerned. Somehow, after the third or fourth replay, we all seem to kid ourselves that the ref was so obviously in the wrong that we spotted it at the time! And yet it is less than routine for reporters to spot errors at the exact second they occur. We usually cover ourselves by inserting a question mark before checking the replay.

It's such a reflex action that when I go to a game as a spectator I'm looking all over the place for a screen to see incidents again. Realising I can't makes me appreciate the predicament of the officials. Television viewers—and not just studio pundits—are now virtually programmed to wait for a rerun before deciding the rights and wrongs of an incident. Only then does it become an 'obvious mistake' by the ref.

Here's a recent personal experience, told at my own expense, which shows why I often feel I'm on the same wavelength. It occurred in September, 2010 while covering a Blackburn-Fulham game for *Final Score*. Mark Schwarzer was having a nightmare in Fulham's goal under an aerial assault from Sam Allardyce's side. Schwarzer came to meet another high ball, got into a tangle and tumbled over, allowing Chris Samba to head into an empty net. Partly because his judgment had previously been so faulty, I decided on the basis of one, split second view of the incident— unwisely because it is better to be circumspect—that the goal was the keeper's fault.

What I couldn't see prior to my instant report was the close-up replay afforded to presenter Gabby Logan and her studio pundits

Garth Crooks and Mark Bright. This clearly showed Schwarzer being unfairly impeded by a challenge from Blackburn's El-Hadji Diouf which meant the goal should have been disallowed by referee Anthony Taylor—whereas I had suspected Schwarzer of running into his own defenders in a crowded area.

Two lessons here. The first is that I should have been more cautious, especially as I was viewing from a distance. The boys in the studio quite rightly corrected me—and this cuts both ways because they are never slow, either, to say the reporter was 'spot on' in other circumstances. The second conclusion is that the live reporter/commentator has to make a similar split-second call to the referee. And if Taylor had a bad day at Ewood Park then so did yours truly. I joined him behind the sofa in watching *Match of the Day* that night!

As a matter of interest, I checked with other broadcasters to see if they had correctly judged the sequence of events in real time. Not one of them was aware an offence had taken place. Yet by the end, all of us were glibly referring to a blunder by ref Taylor as if it was the most obvious thing in the world. Yes, it was blatant—if you studied it again in slow-motion. So, if we are honest, we should give the officials a little more understanding on occasions. But it's interesting to note that they are not the only ones to suffer. I like to think that, by my previous standards over many years, it was an isolated blunder. Taylor returned to the Premier League after serving a short penance. I'm still waiting at the time of writing! Not that I'm complaining after being kept gainfully employed in the Championship. I mention this because the petulant players could learn something from referees—and even journalists—about accepting authority and simply working hard to get back in the 'first team'.

19

REGRETS TOO FEW TO MENTION . . .

John Barnwell, the former chief executive of the League Managers Association, has been another key contact and very highly valued. For more than a decade, John helped me fill the earning void created by the decline of clubs in the Yorkshire area. My dad took a keen interest in this link because, as a lifelong Arsenal fan, he remembered Barnwell playing for the Gunners. As with so many connections, the alliance was formed entirely by chance. It happened because I had done a feature in the *Mail* cataloguing the disgraceful level of abuse suffered by a footballing friend, Terry Dolan, while managing Hull City in the mid-1990s.

John happened to read it. He rang me expressing appreciation and also offered some quotes in support of Terry. It was our first conversation but I immediately sensed that John was one of football's genuine good guys and someone with whom I should try establishing an ongoing relationship. From that day, we spoke regularly and he would entrust me with many confidential insights that I always kept secret. In among them would be the occasional nugget which, on an unattributable basis, could be used. John also opened a wider network of contacts that, for instance, enabled me to break a story, weeks in advance, that Dennis Wise would be sacked by Millwall within months of leading them to the FA Cup final in 2004. There was also a threat by Sir Bobby Robson to sue former club Newcastle and a revelation in 2005 that Oxford United's Argentinean manager Ramon Diaz had been deported.

John, once the manager of many clubs including Wolves, was fiercely protective of his members and would always use his media contacts, including myself, in their best interests. He set up a much-needed health scheme for managers after Joe Kinnear suffered a heart attack while in charge of Wimbledon and also established a university training course for young bosses. I am particularly grateful to John for bringing me into the fold at various annual awards dinners of the LMA. These are pinch-yourself occasions at which you rub shoulders with the likes of Sir Alex (ironically, perhaps, in some circumstances) and Fabio Capello. Naturally, these dinners are also a good fishing ground for freelances.

But, most of all, you just can't beat that Saturday afternoon three o'clock feeling. Whether you are a player, manager, referee or a pampered paid observer, it's like Christmas Day falling every weekend in winter. Except this has, of course, become a moveable feast with all manner of kick-off times to suit television. A pity, I feel, that the fare has become so spread — because too much of what you fancy can kill your appetite.

Hence, there are very few live games on the box that are a must to watch . . . if you are to have a life, that is. But football has been fantastic to me and I try to remember this every time I'm tempted to moan at some minor inconvenience or other. Like any job, there is an element of tedium and a degree of stress. Overworking might seem a desirable hardship but it is also a real hazard for a freelance. You have to take the work when it is there and dread letting in a rival. There have been times when I have become spaced out without realising it — only to discover that my occasional insomnia really has nothing to do with an inability to sleep and is actually caused by not switching off from work. And if your job is a hobby, then really you have no release from it.

But these are insignificant gripes and I was never happier than during my prolonged spell as a regular for 5 Live. I would cover 70-

odd games a season for them at one point, quite often three in a week. And my travels would take me all over the country. There was even a puzzling period when I became Gillingham correspondent. This is a round trip of some 430 miles, but I would try to make a point of keeping the surprise out of my voice when asked to go to the Priestfield Stadium on a Tuesday night, as happened on several occasions.

Bear in mind, I would already have spent most of the day on the story trail and would then have to get up early the next morning to take the kids to school. But the expenses were decent and, even when faced with these, the BBC didn't seem to have much grasp of geography when it came to plotting my next assignment. One week, I did a round trip to Bristol Rovers on the Tuesday and a similar excursion to and from Cambridge United the following night. Sometimes I would go to Norwich or Ipswich. But I had a policy of not turning games down—there is always that nagging fear of someone else getting the job *and* doing it better.

I never took any of the work for granted, especially as I'd often find myself working alongside household names. There was a spell when Trevor Brooking and Gary Lineker were hosting the midweek shows on 5 Live. It was somewhat unreal being handed-to by these former England greats, though I'd met Lineker on a couple of occasions. Once, after he'd scored a hat-trick for Spurs at Hillsborough, I needed to get him up to the press box for a live chat down the line with Saturday presenter John Inverdale. Naturally, he didn't want to plough through fans in the concourse and the only way was to smuggle him up via the no-go area of the directors box. I think he was more worried about being caught than I was! The identity of another celebrity presenter at 5 Live from that era enabled me to boast that I had been on 'Parkinson'. I'll always remember the look of surprise on a press box colleague's face when he heard me in conversation with the presenter during a match and asked: 'Who's Michael?' It's an illusion of radio that you can appear to be matey with someone you have never even met.

It was a jolt when economies bit and, along with several other freelances, I was apologetically removed from the 5 Live roster in 2005—pending a fortunate 'free transfer' to *Final Score*. One happy spin-off was getting to know some of the radio colleagues you never got to meet because you were always spread around.

Like Stuart Hall, for instance. Having been hooked on *It's a Knockout* as a kid, Stuart held a fascination for me. Now I see him regularly and, as the BBC broadcast points are next to each other, I've come to know him as great company. The fun and mischief are still there at a very youthful 81 despite his addiction to the weed—which is something I'm a little ashamed to admit sharing, even though I've rationed down to a few small cigars a day. I've long become conditioned to not smoking at football grounds, where to light up is to risk ejection. But Stuart somehow gets away with it at some unnamed venues! He has a knack for smoking undetected with hand under desk—as if he has his own portable bikeshed with him.

One Saturday at Wigan's JJB Stadium, (now the DW Stadium but then named after the sportswear manufacturers for whom Hall fronted adverts), the game reached half-time and Stuart turned to me. 'Cup of tea, Biggsy?' he asked.

'Yes, good idea—where do we go?' I said, not familiar with the lie of the land.

'Well, I don't know about you,' he said. 'But I'm going down to the boardroom!'

Stuart has this sense of theatre which makes his reporting so iconic. I am the proud owner of a signed script for one of his famed *Sports Report* pieces. It's actually just a scrawl, written in haste and barely legible, on a scrap of paper (and I suspect he has done some of them on a fag packet). But I feel this will be worth something to a suitable charity one day.

Thanks to *Final Score* and programme bosses like Lance Hardy, Mark Demuth and now Ron Chakraborty, I have made a pretty seamless transition to television. Particular thanks to Lance who was the editor who brought me onto the programme after I lost my regular position with 5 Live. So I still get my Saturday kicks, often with newspaper work thrown in. And I keep across the local scene by writing on both clubs for the *Sheffield Telegraph*, thanks initially to Peter Markie who introduced me during the 1990s and latterly to editorial pair David Todd and Derek Fish. So it's a great life and the many good years have gone a long way towards securing my family's future, along, I should add, with my wife's job as a teacher. Not that it has quenched my appetite for more of the action because money has never been my god. I remember David Pleat saying to me once that the real joy was simply being involved in the game, nothing more.

I don't have any regrets—even when World Cups come along and friends ask me why I'm not out there. This irritates after a while because only the top-liners get to go and usually they are either staffers or on full-time contracts. And I wish I could get away from the perpetual question about what I do in summer (which, among other things, happens to have been writing this book).

But I don't wonder too much about what would have happened if I had taken the various jobs that have kindly been offered to me. In the case of the first, with *Today* newspaper, my decision proved to be inspired in that the paper closed shortly afterwards . . . although the guy they went for did end up as a national columnist! Maybe I was wrong, after all. It's Des Kelly, now of the *Daily Mail*, by the way. For me, the main issue was that there would have been no scope to continue my BBC work and I couldn't give that up.

Later I was approached by an old Hallam colleague, Nick Atkins, who was in a senior position at Sky. He asked if I'd be interested in becoming a football reporter for the network and at first it seemed like the opportunity I'd been waiting for. But it was to cover a mighty strip of country between Nottingham and Newcastle—for less money than I was earning self-employed. Even then, I was quite keen but the lack of a company car nailed the dream. My kids were young then and I realised I'd hardly see them.

Actually watching them grow up, while a distraction at times, has been one of the beauties of my lifestyle. That said, sacrifice goes hand in hand with ambition and I've often longed to do more television work.

I guess I've been happy with my lot. But one decision, well before these, was almost certainly misguided. Working as Hallam's sports editor in around 1982, I was stunned one day to receive a phone call in the office from Radio Sheffield's manager, Tim Pitt. Bold as brass, he said he was looking for a sports editor and he thought I was 'eminently suitable'. I was so flattered by this I could hardly get my head through the various doors to sprinkle the gossip around the station.

In truth, I was more tickled by the approach, and the directness of it, than pleased to be offered the job. I did visit Tim Pitt for a chat but my mind was virtually made up. At Hallam, we were hitting the local rivals for six with our vibrant brand of broadcasting, not least in sport. Radio Sheffield, by comparison at the time, seemed very pedestrian and dull and I doubted whether I would have much impact in livening it up, regardless of how I operated on sport. But on reflection this was a mistake. There were few career outlets in commercial radio whereas the BBC offered immeasurable scope. If there is one decision I would probably change it is that one. And besides, Radio Sheffield now hold a virtual monopoly on local sports broadcasting with very comprehensive coverage that commands large audiences.

My only other regret is that, in common with a good many first-time authors of my age, I wish my parents could have been around to see their son on the bookshelves. Alas, my mum was taken by cancer in 1988 and my dad passed away a few years ago. I'm sure they would have been as proud of me as I still am of them.

In every other respect, I'm just pleased to have made a go of it for so long. I've had variety too, working as a journalist and broadcaster, and gained a lot of experience in both fields. That, combined with the enthusiasm I still feel, is why I'm confident of new chapters to come. But, whatever happens from here, I'm so lucky to have had so much fun while making a living—and to have accumulated such a collection of stories involving household names. It comes to quite a bundle. Thank you for letting me drop it in your lap!

FONDLY REMEMBERED

Working friends and colleagues with whom I would love to have shared this book:

Audrey Adams, Graham Bannister, John Brand, Graham Chatfield, Derrick Connolly, Peter Cooper, Jean Doyle, Jim Greensmith, Benny Hill, David Jones, Dave Kilner, Simon Meeks, Roger Moffat, Tony Pritchett, Martin Searby, Ray Stuart, Alan Thompson, Bridget Whittaker, Bruce Wyndham.